John R. Sweney

Radiant Songs

For use in meetings for Christian worship or work

John R. Sweney

Radiant Songs
For use in meetings for Christian worship or work

ISBN/EAN: 9783337038175

Printed in Europe, USA, Canada, Australia, Japan

Cover: Foto ©Lupo / pixelio.de

More available books at **www.hansebooks.com**

RADIANT SONGS:

FOR USE IN

MEETINGS FOR CHRISTIAN WORSHIP OR WORK.

EDITORS:

JNO. R. SWENEY, WM. J. KIRKPATRICK, AND H. L. GILMOUR.

"Upon them hath the light shined."
—Is. ix. 2.

PHILADELPHIA:
Published by JOHN J. HOOD, 1024 Arch St.

Copyright, 1891, by John J. Hood.

RADIANT with light the bending skies,
With radiant hope earth is aglow;
And joy to radiant joy replies,
As skies resmile in lakes below.

So radiant hearts to hearts unfold,
So radiant hope keeps life aflame;
So "Radiant Songs," the heart's best gold,
Shall gladden earth with Jesus' name.

Ocean Grove, N. J., June, 1891.   E. H STOKES.

COPYRIGHT NOTICE.

To PRINT, for sale or otherwise, any copyright hymn of this collection, unless written permission shall have been obtained, is an infringement of copyright.

THE PUBLISHER.

Rejoice in the Lord.

Mrs. E. E. Williams. Psalm 33. H. L. Gilmour.

1. Rejoice in the Lord, O ye upright of heart, Sing praise to his excellent name; his name,
2. Rejoice in the Lord, in a new, happy song, The song of redemption so sweet; so sweet,
3. Rejoice in the Lord, the Redeemer of men, His life for a ransom he gave, he gave,
4. Rejoice in the Lord, for his work is complete, Salvation to all he doth bring; doth bring,
5. Rejoice in the Lord, for he cometh again, By seraphs and angels adored, adored,

With songs of salvation, with timbrel and harp, His mercy and goodness proclaim.
Let mountains and valleys the ech- o prolong, And nations the chorus repeat.
Re - joice, for he liveth again, Victorious o'er death and the grave.
Ye isles of the ocean, come bow at his feet, And crown him your Saviour and King.
Come, all ye redeemed ones, unite in the strain, Rejoice, as ye watch for the Lord!

CHORUS. *Allegro.*

Re- joice, re - joice, re - joice,   Tri- um - phantly sing,

re - joice, re - joice, tri - um- phant- ly we'll sing, O sing,

Rejoice, rejoice, re- joice,   In Je - sus our King; Let the whole earth re-

re- joice, rejoice,

spond, in a might- y acclaim, All glo - ry and praise to his ex - cellent name.

Copyright, 1891, by H. L. Gilmour.

Glory, I'm Redeemed.

F. A. B.
F. A. BLACKMER.

1. On the Saviour I've believed, Gracious pardon I've received, And his
2. When I heard his loving voice, How it made my heart rejoice, Like sweet
3. All a-long my pil-grim way I will trust him and o-bey, And each
4. Wondrous comfort does he send, Proving such a constant friend, For he

blood now covers all my guilt and shame; In my soul to dwell he deigns, Without
music to my longing soul it came; Oh, how wondrous, full and free, Was his
day I'll seek to spread my Saviour's fame; To ex-alt, my aim shall be, Him who
comes to bless in ev'ry need the same; Empty turns me not a-way, But new

ri - val there he reigns, Glo - ry, glo - ry, hal-le - lu - jah to his name!
pard'ning love to me! Glo - ry, glo - ry, hal-le - lu - jah to his name!
did so much for me, Glo - ry, glo - ry, hal-le - lu - jah to his name!
blessings sends each day, Glo - ry, glo - ry, hal-le - lu - jah to his name!

CHORUS.

I'm redeemed, I'm redeemed, In his power the Saviour came, And from sin gave
I'm redeemed, I'm redeemed, hallelujah, sweet re-

lease, Filled my soul with heav'nly peace, Glory, glory, hallelujah to his name!

Copyright, 1891, by John J. Hood.

Lay Aside Thy Fears.—CONCLUDED. 11

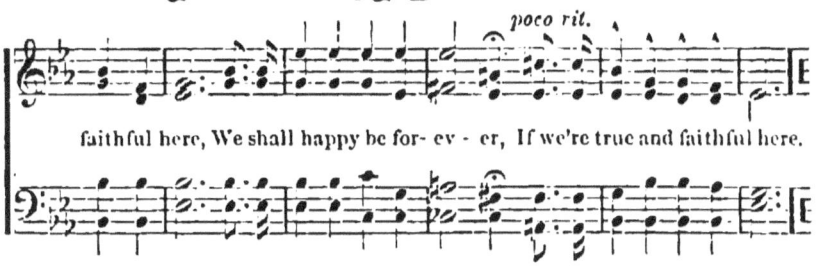

faithful here, We shall happy be for-ev - er, If we're true and faithful here.

Live it Out.

L. H. EDMUNDS. JNO. R. SWENEY.

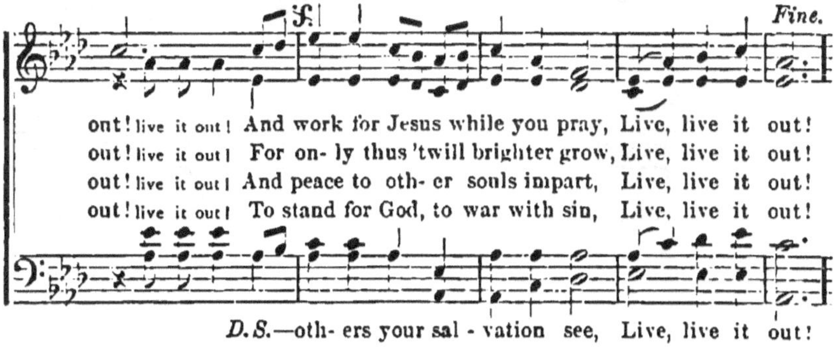

1. How - ev - er weak your faith to-day, Live it out, live it out, live it
2. The love that burns with fit-ful glow, Live it out, live it out, live it
3. The truth you hold within your heart, Live it out, live it out, live it
4. The power the Spir - it gives within, Live it out, live it out, live it

Fine.

out! live it out! And work for Jesus while you pray, Live, live it out!
out! live it out! For on-ly thus 'twill brighter grow, Live, live it out!
out! live it out! And peace to oth-er souls impart, Live, live it out!
out! live it out! To stand for God, to war with sin, Live, live it out!

D.S.—oth-ers your sal - vation see, Live, live it out!

CHORUS. D. S.

O, let your life a witness be That Christ our Lord has made you free, Let

Copyright, 1891, by Jno. R. Sweney.

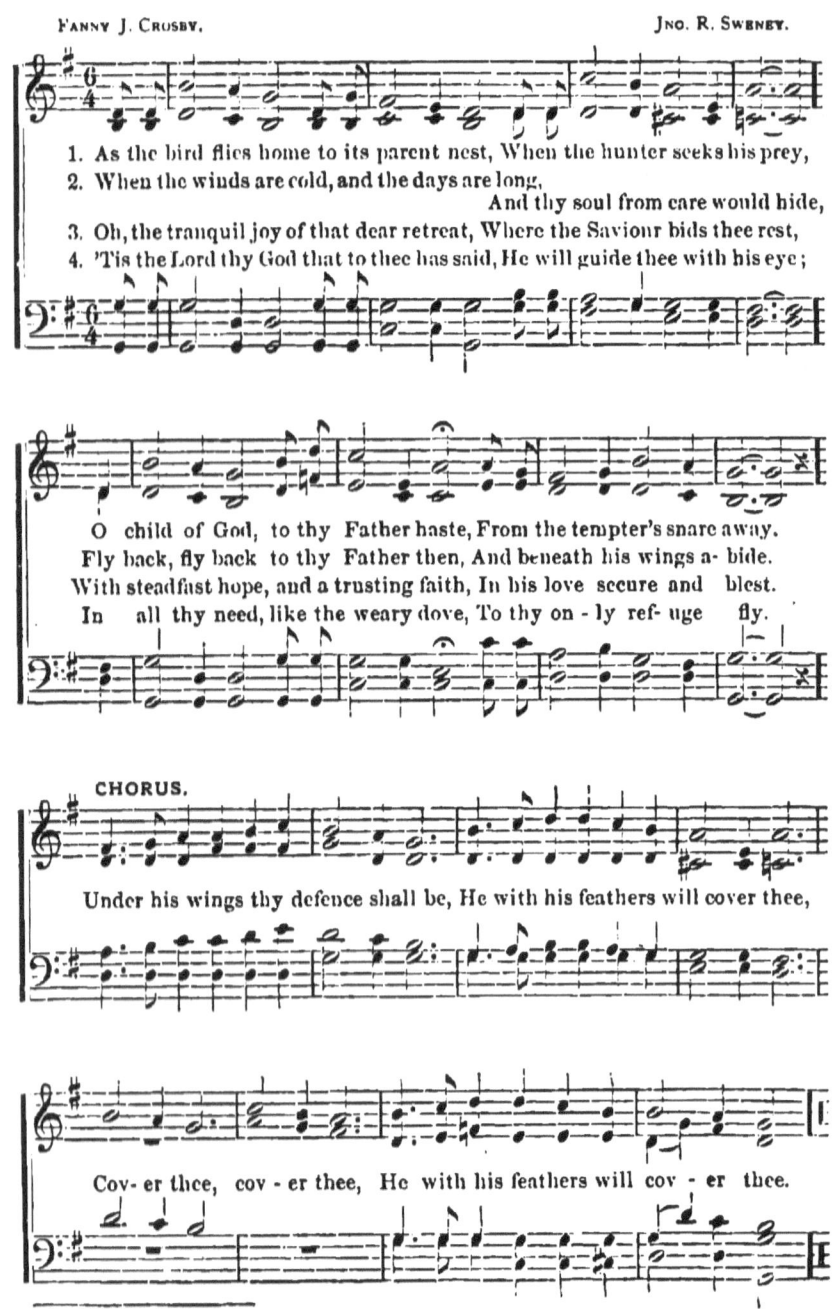

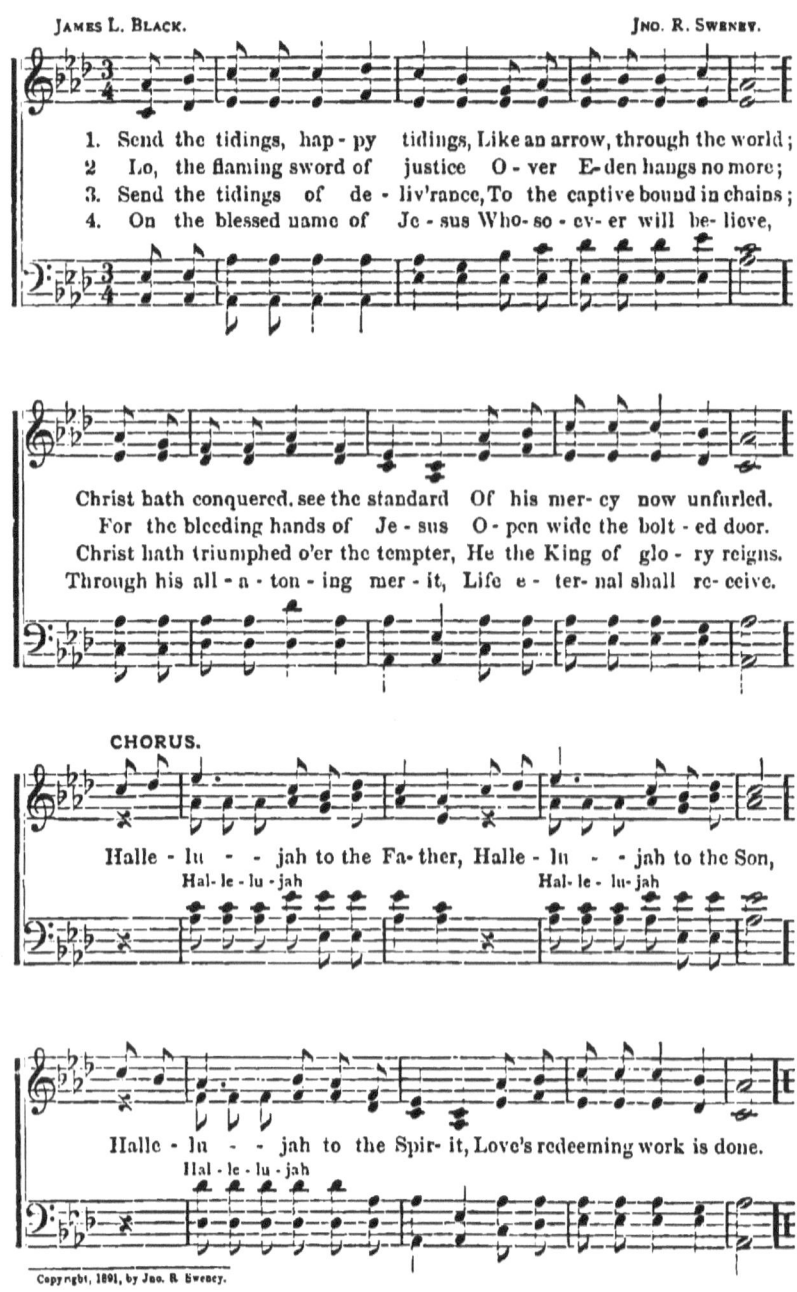

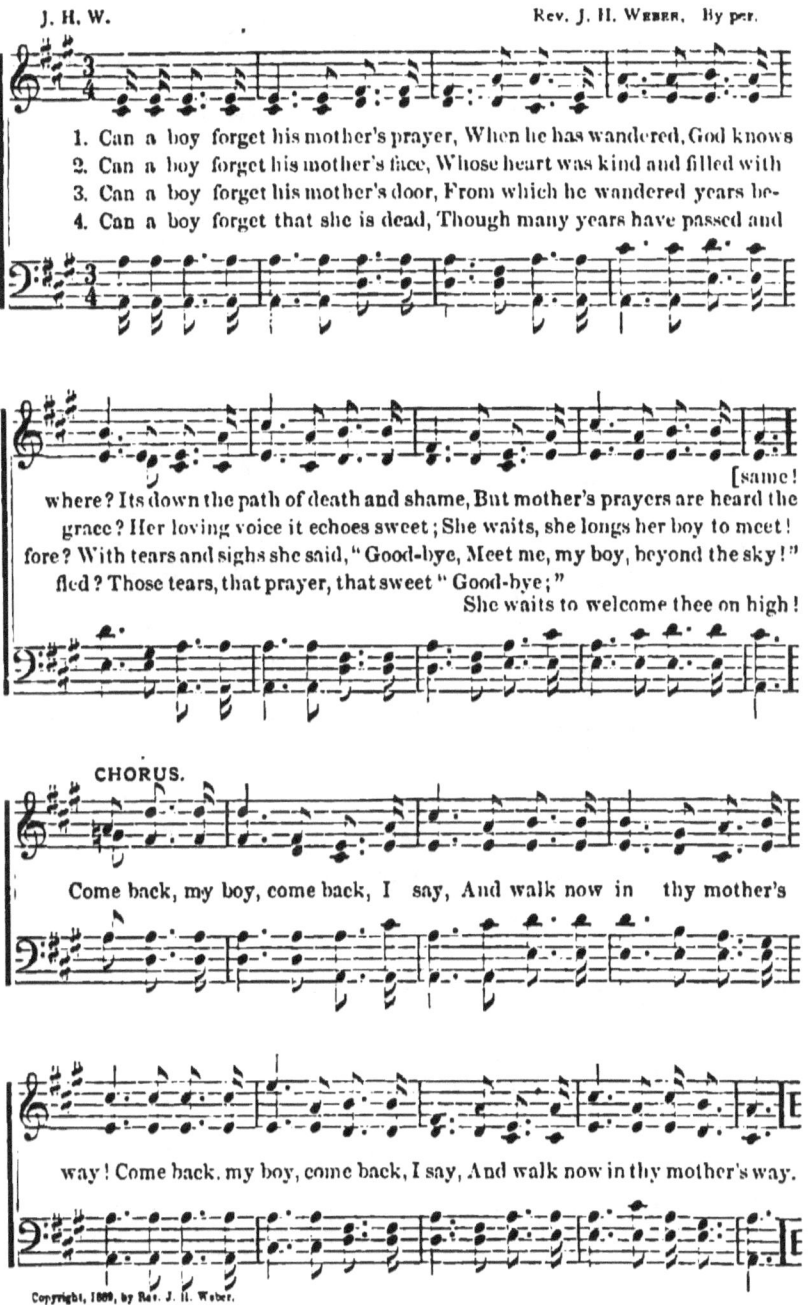

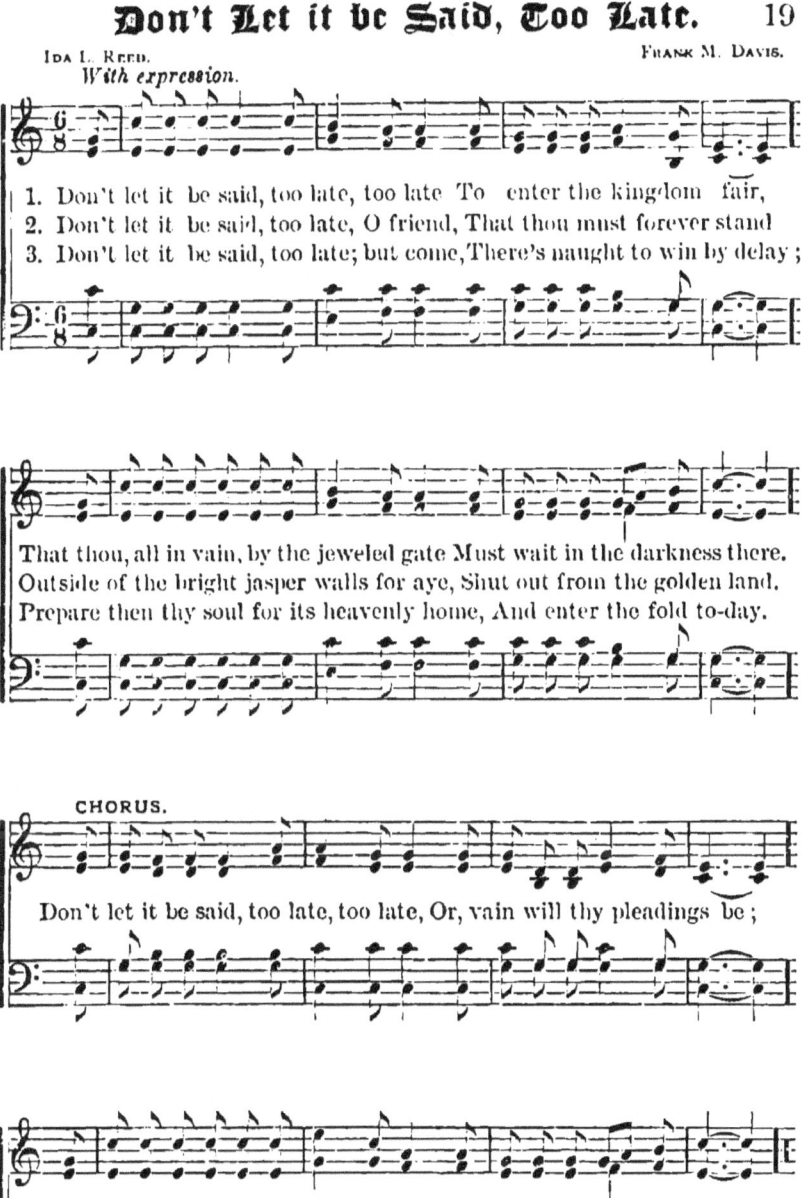

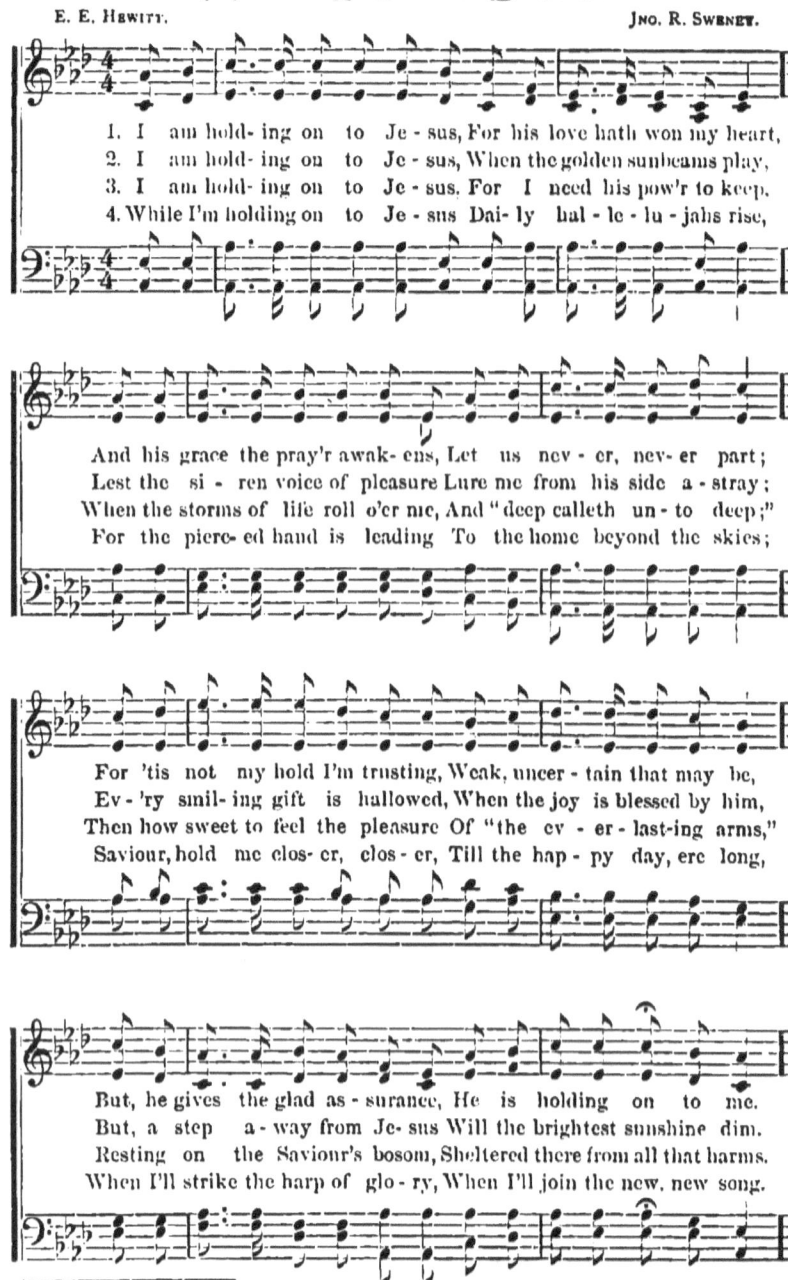

Holding On to Jesus.—CONCLUDED.

Peace, Said the Master.

L. H. EDMUNDS.   "Peace I leave with you."—John xiv: 27.   WM. J. KIRKPATRICK.

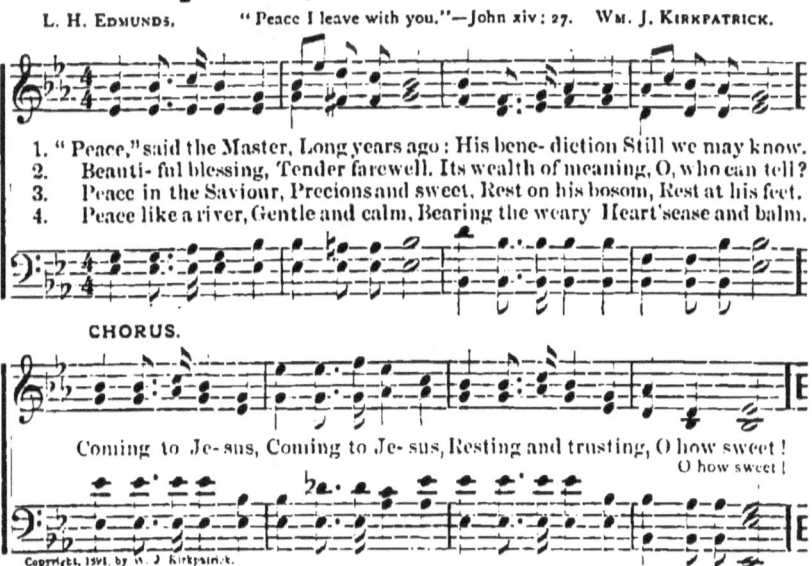

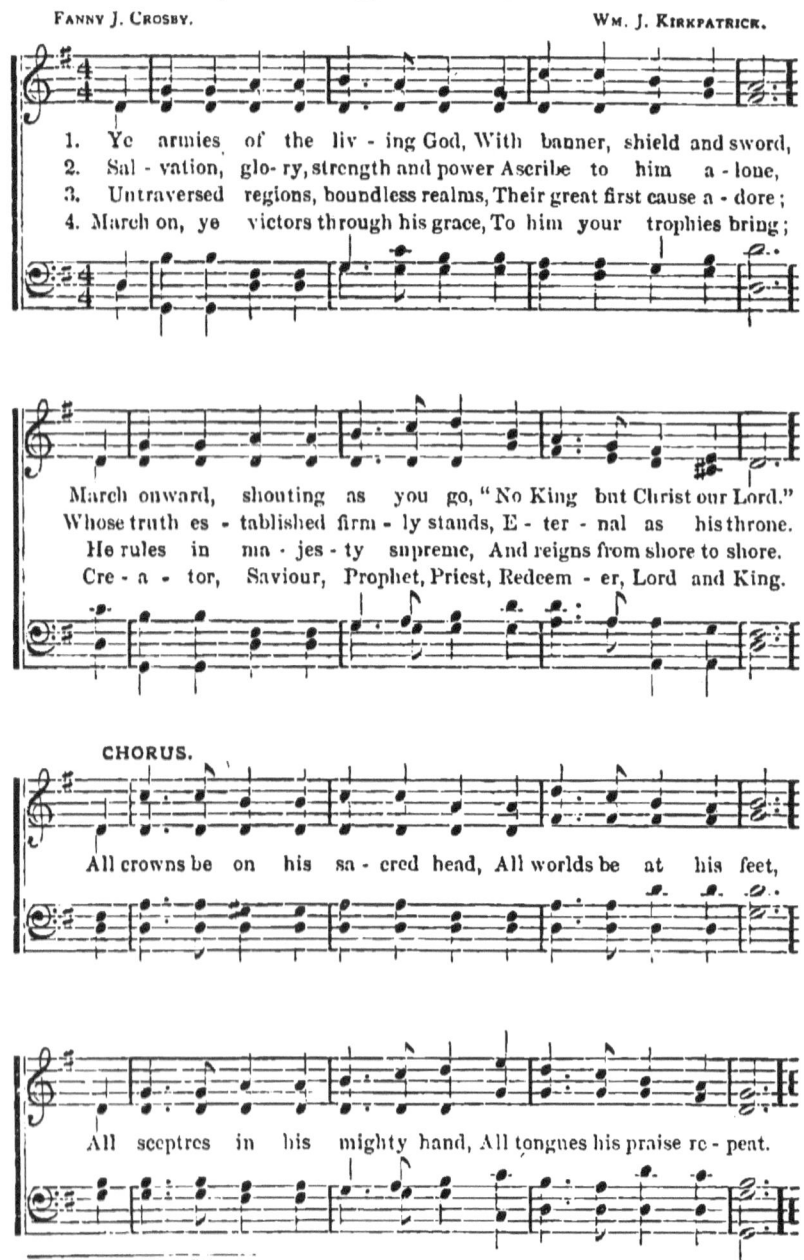

The Morning Light.

A. S. Kieffer. D. E. Dortch.

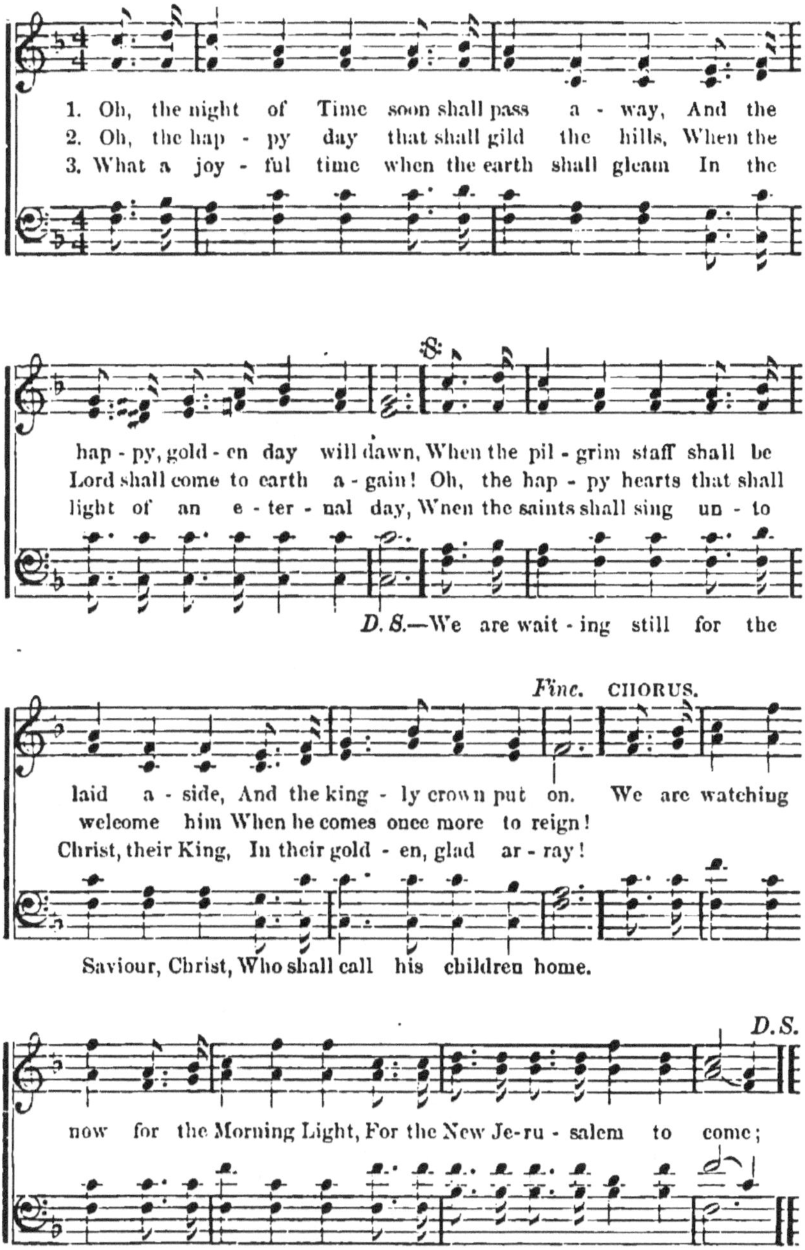

From "Grace and Glory," by per.

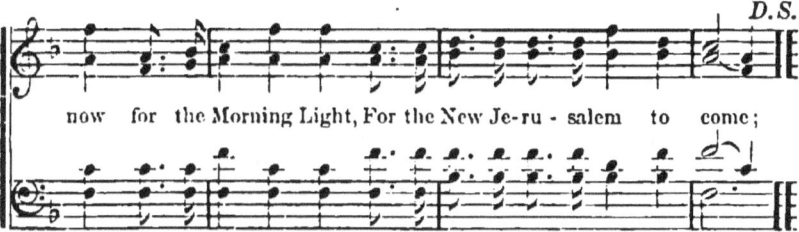

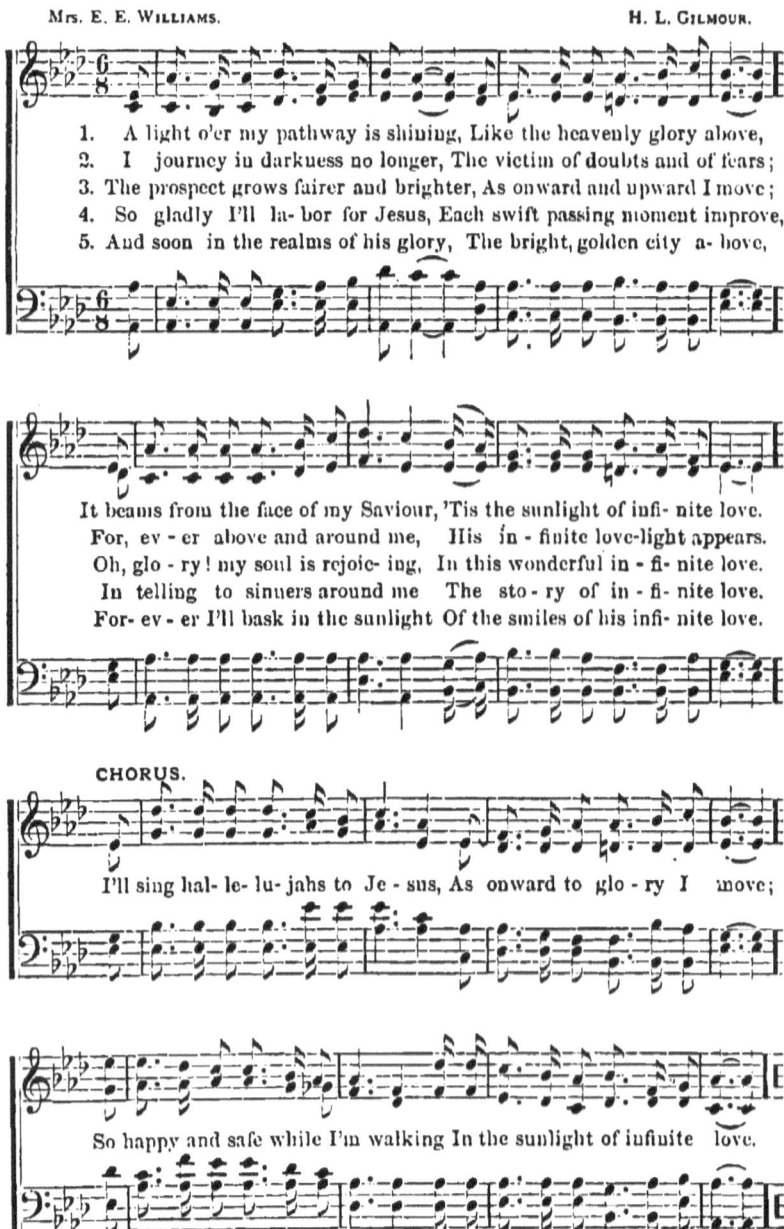

Hasten Thy Kingdom.—CONCLUDED.

All tongues confess him, The world his name adore, The world his name adore.
his name a-dore

All for Jesus.

MARY D. JAMES.
JNO. R. SWENEY.

1. All for Je-sus! all for Je-sus! All my being's ransomed powers:
2. Let my hands perform his bidding, Let my feet run in his ways—
3. Worldlings prize their gems of beauty, Cling to gild-ed toys of dust,
4. Since my eyes were fixed on Je-sus, I've lost sight of all be-sides;
5. Oh, what wonder! how a-mazing! Je-sus, glorious King of kings—

S.   *Fine.*

All my thoughts, and words, and doings, All my days, and all my hours.
Let my eyes see Je-sus on-ly, Let my lips speak forth his praise.
Boast of wealth, and fame, and pleasure: On-ly Je-sus will I trust.
So enchained my spir-it's vis-ion, Looking at the Cru-ci-fied.
Deigns to call me his be-lov-ed, Lets me rest beneath his wings.

D.S.—All for Je-sus! blessed Je-sus! I am his, and he is mine.

CHORUS.   *D.S.*

All for Je-sus! blessed Je-sus! All for Je-sus, gladly I re-sign;

Copyright, 1891, by Jno. R. Sweney.

Brighter Every Day.

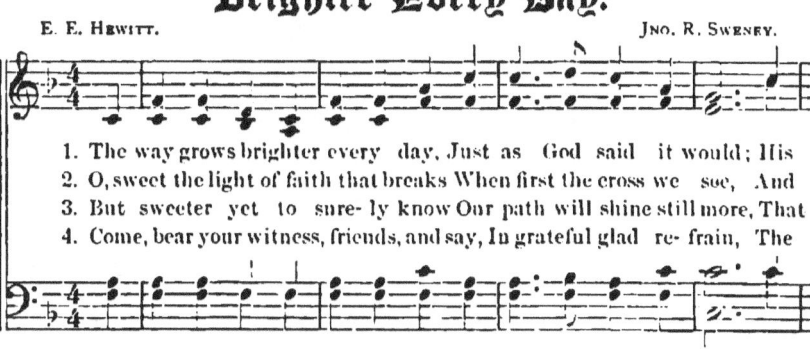

1. The way grows brighter every day, Just as God said it would; His
2. O, sweet the light of faith that breaks When first the cross we see, And
3. But sweeter yet to surely know Our path will shine still more, That
4. Come, bear your witness, friends, and say, In grateful glad refrain, The

CHORUS.

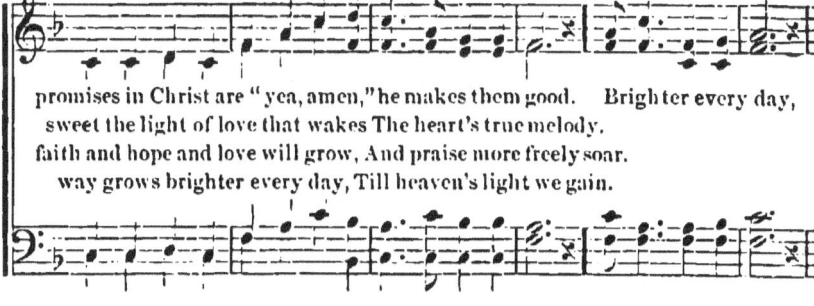

promises in Christ are "yea, amen," he makes them good. Brighter every day,
sweet the light of love that wakes The heart's true melody.
faith and hope and love will grow, And praise more freely soar.
way grows brighter every day, Till heaven's light we gain.

Clearer all the way, The way grows brighter every day, Till heaven's light we gain.

Copyright, 1891, by Jno R Sweney.

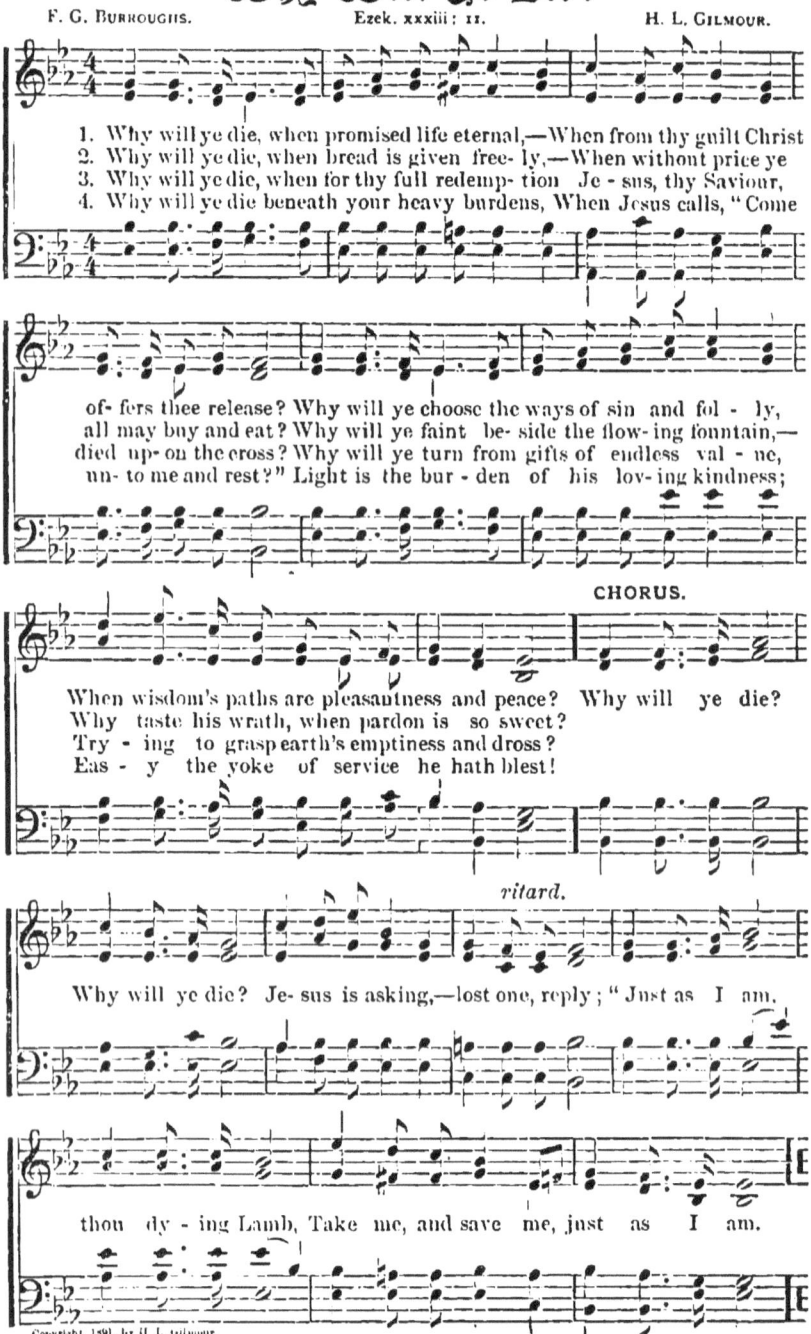

42. Clinging to Thee.

SALLIE MARTIN. JNO. R. SWENEY.

1. Father above, a blessing I seek, Speak to me now, O, tender- ly speak;
2. Saviour divine, whatever betide, Sheltered by thee, O, let me a- bide;
3. Spirit of love, my teacher and friend, Now like a dove, I pray thee, descend;
4. Father above, O Saviour divine, Spirit of love, all worship be thine;

Dark is the way unless thou art near, Yet, with thy presence, no danger I fear.
There I am safe, though surges may roll, Firm is my anchor, O Rock of my soul.
Dwell in my heart, for then shall I sing Praise to my Saviour, Redeemer and King.
Blessed triune, three persons in one, Here as in glory thy will shall be done.

CHORUS.

Cling - - ing to thee, ... cling - - ing to thee,
Clinging to thee, clinging to thee, Clinging to thee, clinging to thee,

No . . . . oth- er ref - uge have I . . . . . . but thee. . . . .
No oth- er ref- uge have I but thee, No oth- er ref- uge have I but thee,

Cling - - ing to thee, ... cling - - ing to thee, ...
Clinging to thee, clinging to thee, Clinging to thee, clinging to thee,

Copyright, 1891, by Jno. R. Sweney.

Clinging to Thee.—CONCLUDED.

Un - - - der thy shad - ow my trust shall ev- er be.....
Un - der thy shad- ow my trust shall ev - er be,

Brought Back.

H. L. GILMOUR.   Arr. by J. J. H.

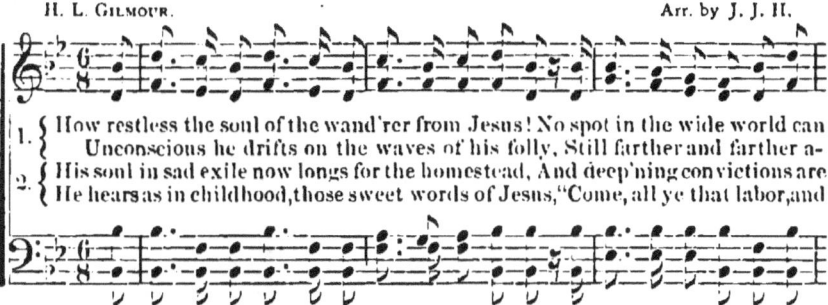

1. How restless the soul of the wand'rer from Jesus! No spot in the wide world can
Unconscious he drifts on the waves of his folly, Still farther and farther
2. His soul in sad exile now longs for the homestead, And deep'ning convictions are
He hears as in childhood, those sweet words of Jesus, "Come, all ye that labor, and

D. C.—And chords of "sweet home," that have long been reposing,
By fingers unseen are a-
D. C. He ventures in weakness, but strength is imparted, And gladly he's welcomed by

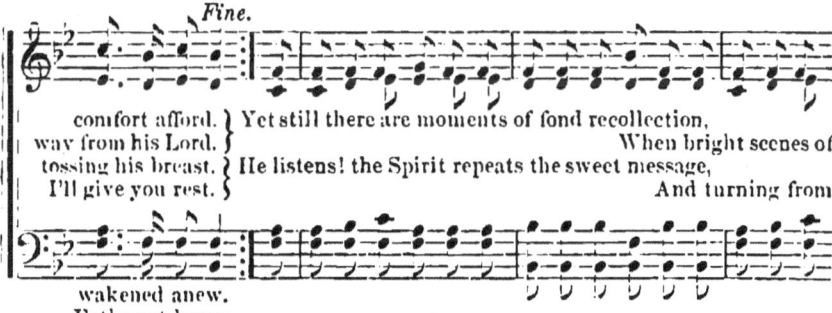

comfort afford. } Yet still there are moments of fond recollection,
way from his Lord. }   When bright scenes of
tossing his breast. } He listens! the Spirit repeats the sweet message,
I'll give you rest. }   And turning from

wakened anew.
Father at home.

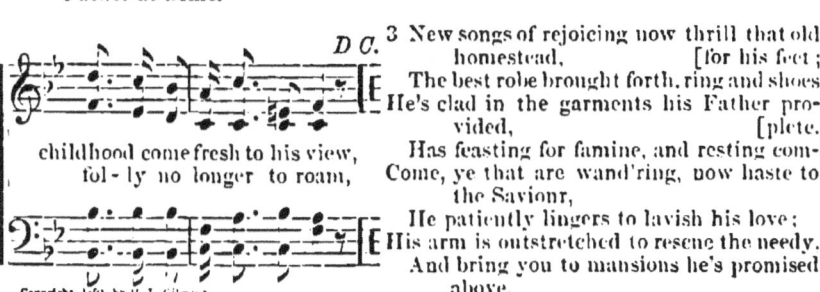

D. C.

childhood come fresh to his view,
fol - ly no longer to roam,

3 New songs of rejoicing now thrill that old
homestead,   [for his feet ;
The best robe brought forth, ring and shoes
He's clad in the garments his Father pro-
vided,   [plete.
Has feasting for famine, and resting com-
Come, ye that are wand'ring, now haste to
the Saviour,
He patiently lingers to lavish his love ;
His arm is outstretched to rescue the needy,
And bring you to mansions he's promised
above.

Copyright, 1891, by H. L. Gilmour.

Sometime.—CONCLUDED.

Beware! beware! At the pearly gate God may answer your sometime, too late! too late!

On to the Battle Front.

LIZZIE EDWARDS.   JNO. R. SWENEY.

1. On to the battle front, Boldly to-day, Boldly to-day;
2. Fight the fight manful - ly, What do ye fear? What do ye fear?
3. Yield not an inch of ground, Though sorely pressed, Though sorely pressed;
4. Think of the crowns of joy Laid up in heav'n, Laid up in heav'n;

CHORUS.

Clad in your armor bright, Soldiers, a - way. Strike at the root of sin,
Wield the sword mightily, Je - sus is near.
Lay not your armor down, Stay not to rest.
Think that to you at last They may be given

Strike in your Leader's name; Vict'ry thro' him proclaim, Soldiers, a-way.

Copyright, 1891, by Jno. R. Sweney.

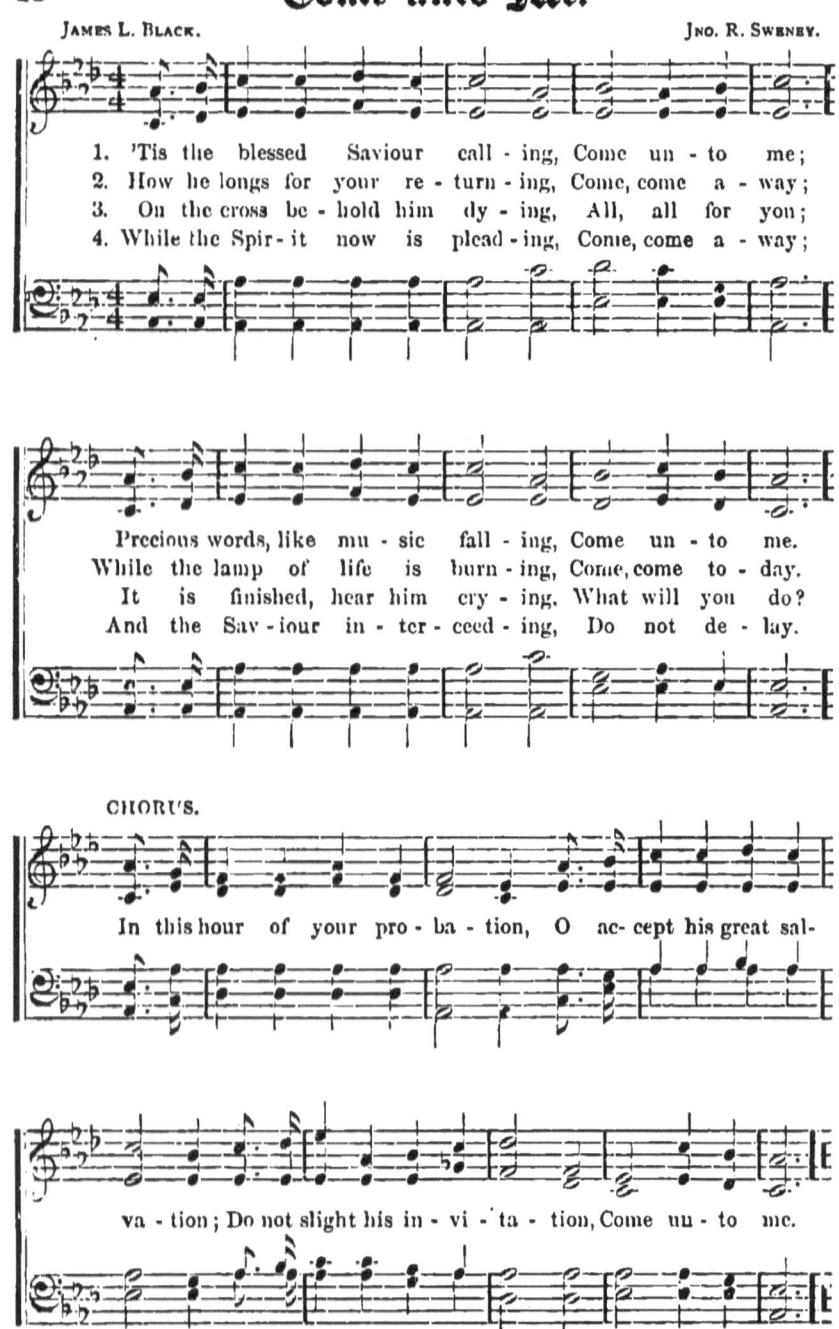

5 E'er again we face the conflict
  Raging in this sinful world,
  Let us sit in sweet communion
  Where love's banner is unfurl'd.

6 Till our hearts shall burn within us
  Thy salvation to proclaim,
  Then, O Lord, prepare thy servants
  Thus to glorify thy name.

Keep Close to the Rock. 53

"Once more he pressed him tenderly in his arms, saying, Keep close to the Rock, my son, which were his last words."

F. G. BURROUGHS.   H. L. GILMOUR.

1. This life is like a vapor That soon shall pass away, While dangers seen and
2. Although the days are evil, For great is Satan's sway, His snares cannot o'er
3. This Rock shall be our refuge From foes on every hand; This Rock shall be a

unseen Surround our steps each day; But when the death-knell soundeth we
come us While by this Rock we stay; Hosts may encamp against us, Our
shad - ow In earth's sad, weary, land; This rock shall be our shel - ter From

will not dread the shock, If we are ever keeping Close to the Living-Rock.
hearts shall feel no fear If to the Rock, Christ Jesus, We're ever keeping near.
every stormy blast: This Rock shall lead us onward Till all life's ills are past.

CHORUS.

1st.

Keep close, close, close to Christ the Rock, For a-ges it has sheltered and

Keep close, keep close, keep

2d.

borne eve - ry shock, No harm shall e'er befall thee, When close to the Rock.

Copyright, 1891, by H. L. Gilmour.

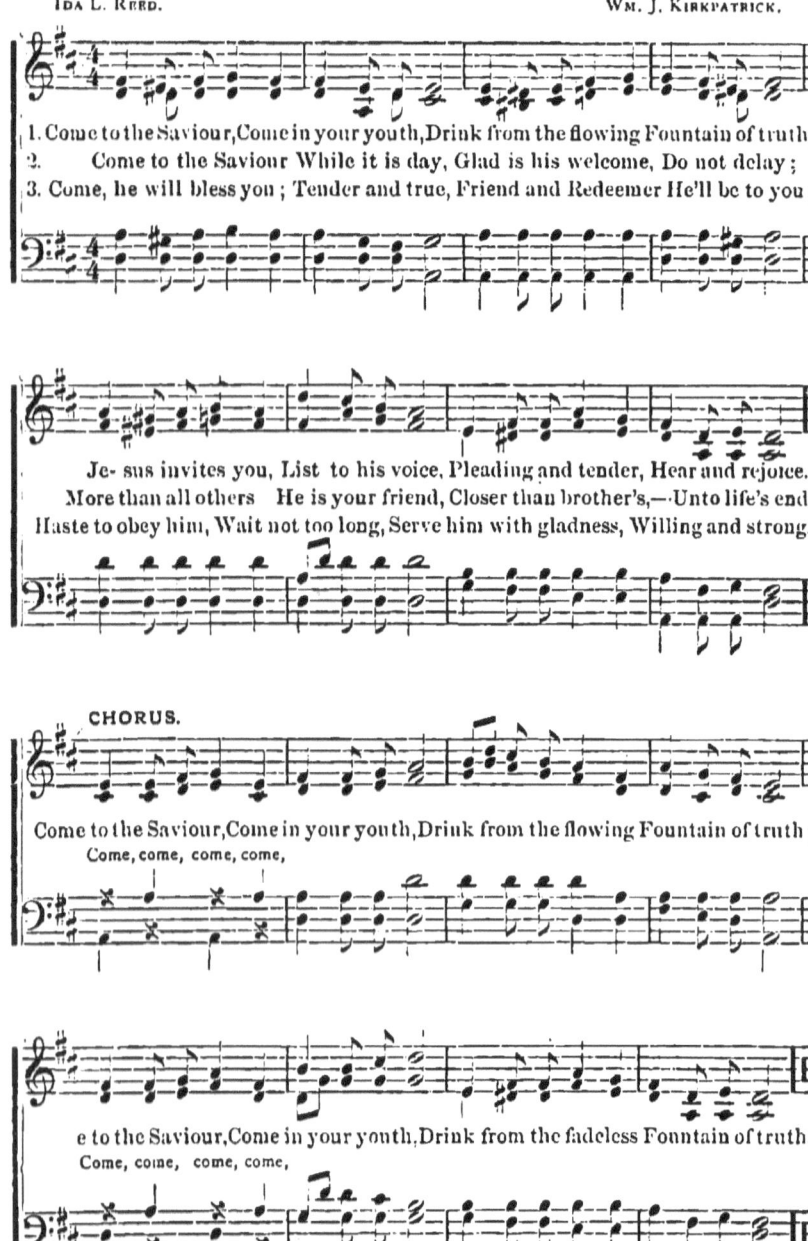

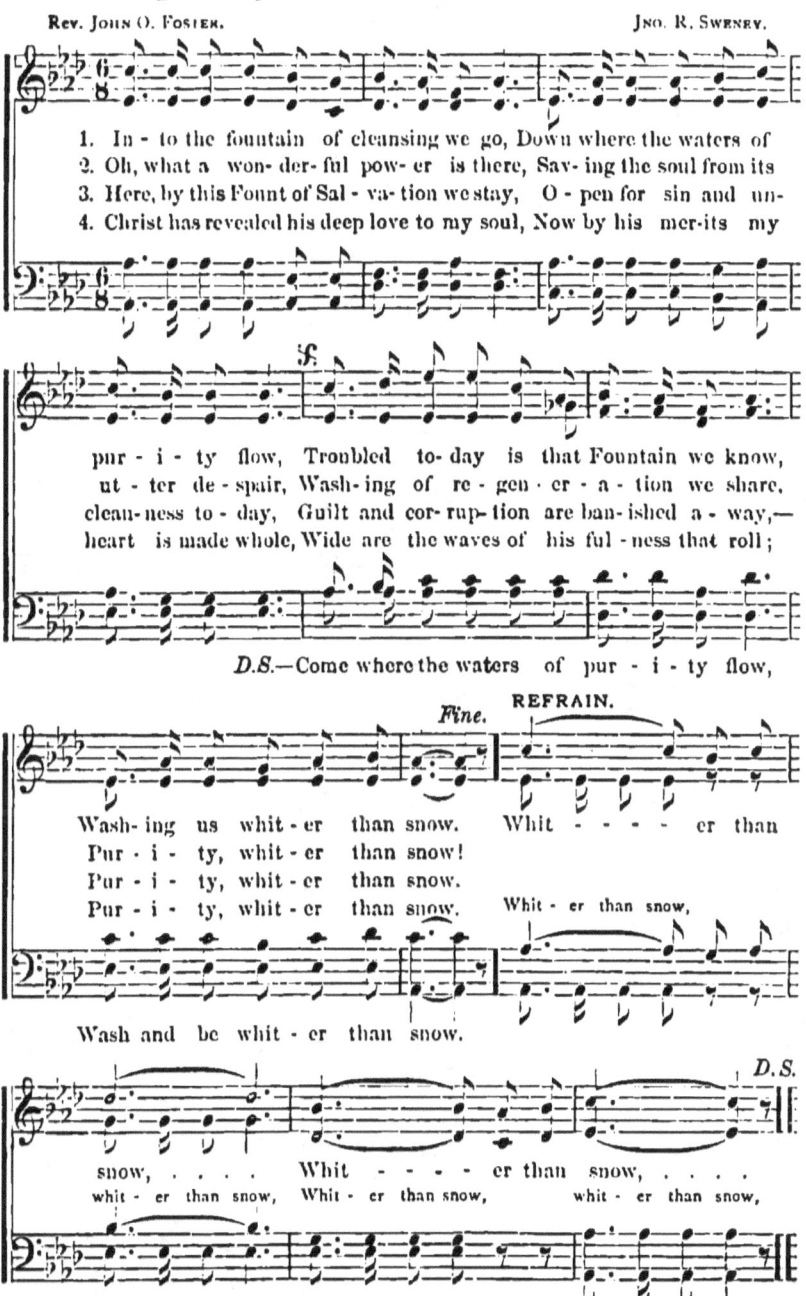

62. Anchored On the Rock of Ages.

F. L. CORNISH.   "This is my Rest forever."—Psalm cxxxii: 14.   JNO. R. SWENEY.

1. Resting in the love of Je - sus, Sweetly rest - - ing
2. I can hear the surges tread - ing Up and down life's
3. Here is ev - - er- lasting com - fort, Here is found the

ev - 'ry day, Anchored on the Rock of A - ges,
storm - y beach, But up - on this sure Founda - tion
sweet - est peace, Here I shall a - bide in pa - tience,

Till the shad - - ows flee a - way.   **CHORUS.**   I am resting, sweetly
I am far beyond their reach.
Till life's storms for - ev - er cease.

resting, Resting, happy, happy all the day, Anchored on . . . the
Anchored on the

Rock of A - ges, Till the shad - - ows flee a - way.
Till the shad - ows

Copyright, 1891, by Jno. R. Sweney.

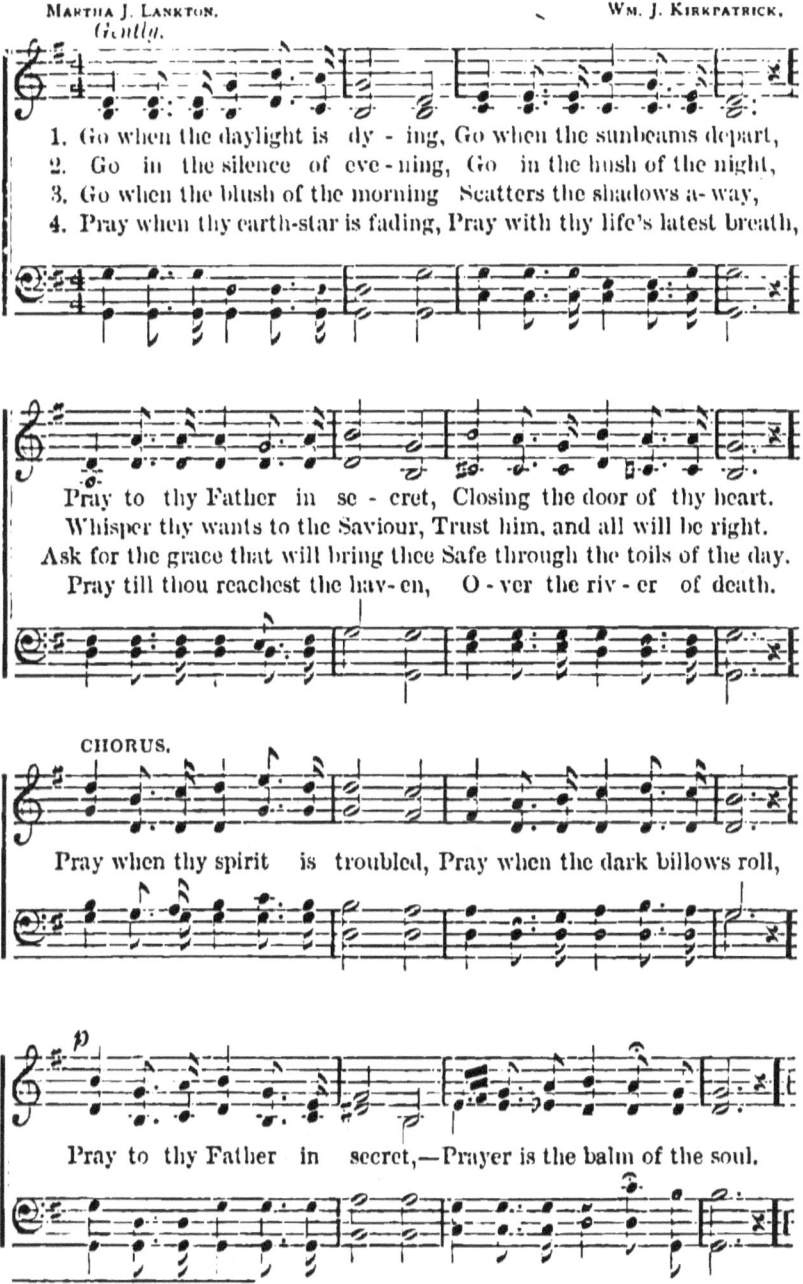

64. O that Beautiful Land so Fair.

WM. STEVENSON. WM. J. KIRKPATRICK.

1. O'er the rapid stream Is a land unseen, And its fields are bright and fair;
2. There is joy for me When that land I see, Dear ones gone before are there;
3. Never-fading flowers Bloom in Eden's bowers, And its charms no tongue can tell;
4. O what joy 'twill be When that home I see, And its glories round me shine;

'Tis the pilgrim's home, Where no sorrows come, And my soul its bliss would share.
By the pearly gate Will they watch and wait, And a joyous welcome bear.
In its glories bright Will my soul delight, And my voice its anthems swell.
When my wond'ring eyes See the promised prize, And a starry crown be mine.

CHORUS.

O that beauti-ful land so fair, Ma-ny loved ones are o-ver there;

How my soul in its bliss would share! Beautiful home in heaven!

Copyright, 1891, by Wm. J. Kirkpatrick.

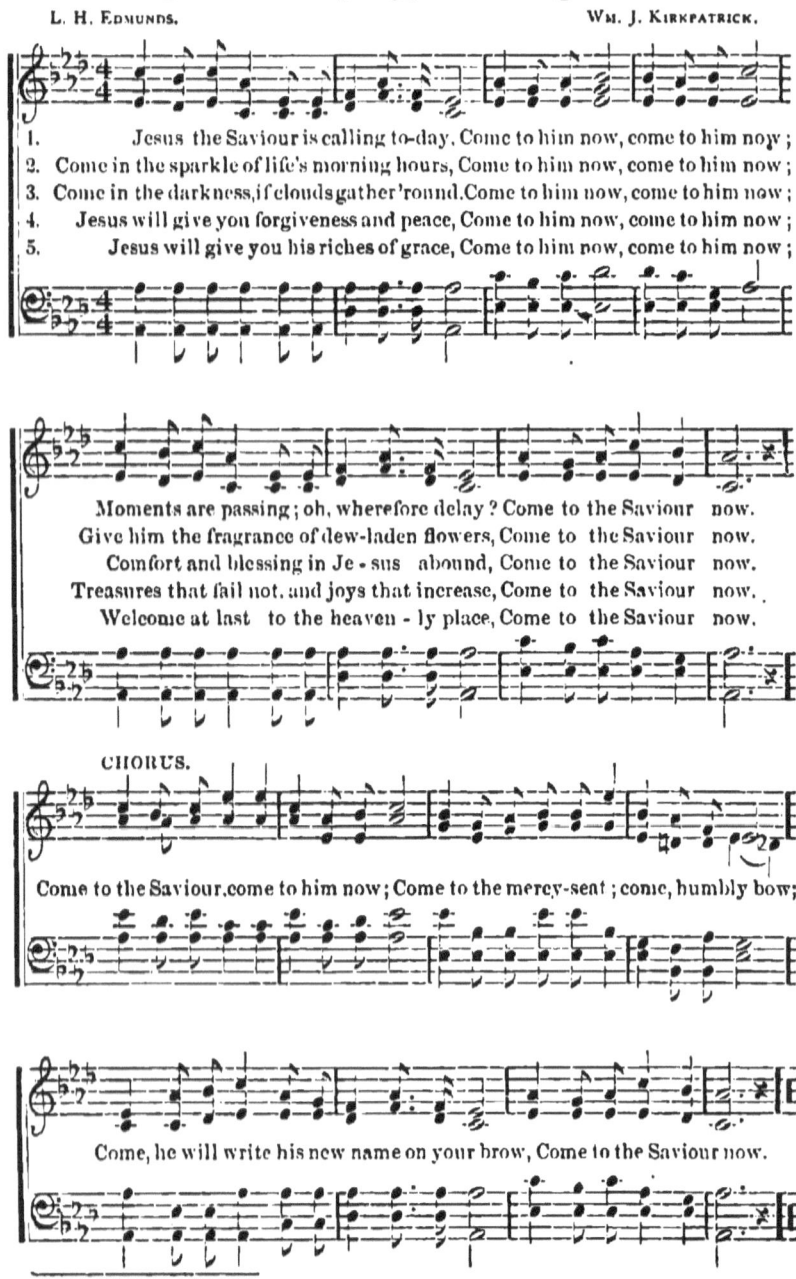

Anywhere With Jesus. 67

JESSIE H. BROWN. "I will trust and not be afraid." Isaiah xii. 2. D. B. TOWNER. By per.

1. An-ywhere with Je-sus I can safe-ly go, An-ywhere He leads me in this world be-low. Anywhere without him, dearest joys would fade, Anywhere with Je-sus I am not a-fraid.
2. An-ywhere with Je-sus I am not a-lone, Other friends may fail me, He is still my own. Tho' his hand may lead me o-ver drearest ways, Anywhere with Je-sus is a house of praise.
3. An-ywhere with Je-sus I can go to sleep, When the darkling shadows round a-bout me creep; Knowing I shall waken nev-er more to roam, Anywhere with Je-sus will be home, sweet home.

CHORUS.

An-y-where! an-y-where! Fear I can-not know,
An-y-where with Je-sus I can safe-ly go.

Copyright, 1887, by D. B. Towner.

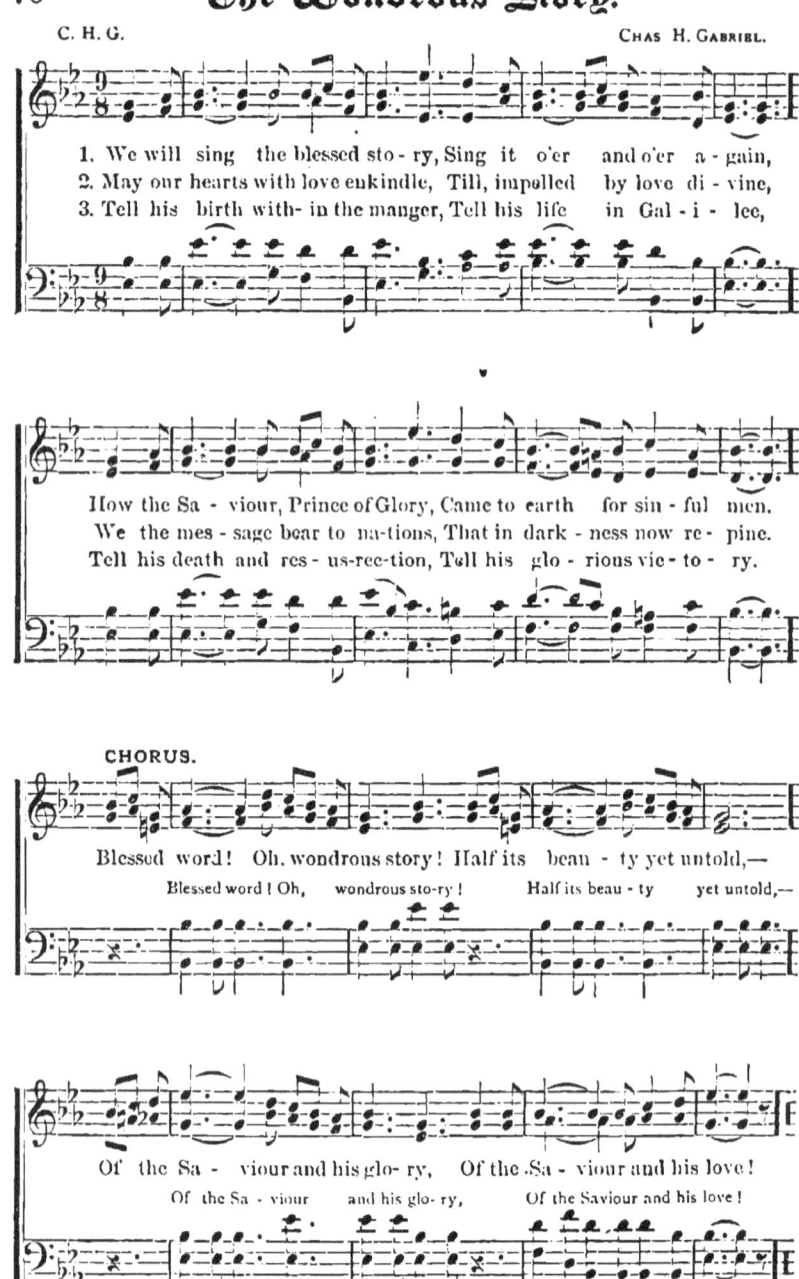

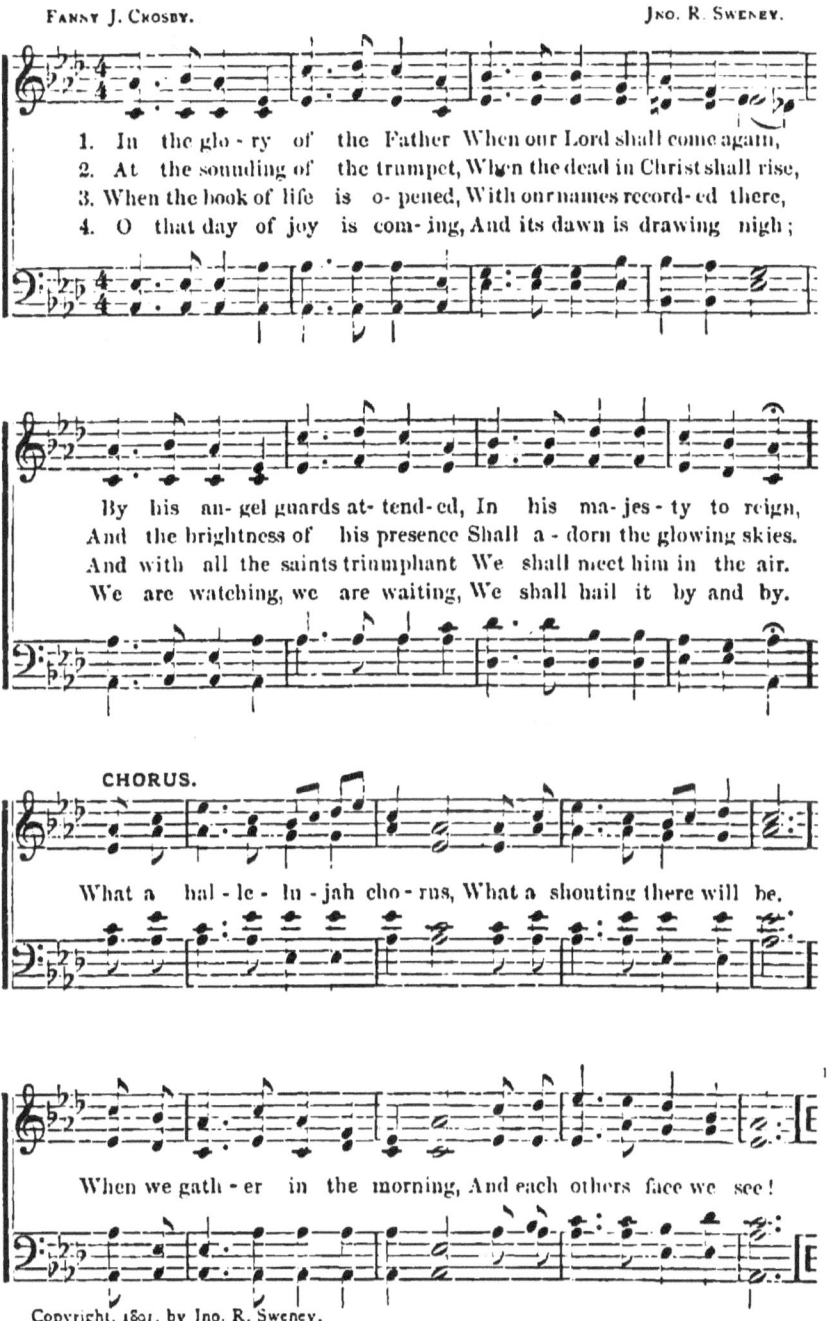

72. Let us Carry the Sunshine.

LIDIE H. EDMUNDS.　　　　　　　　　　　　　　　WM. J. KIRKPATRICK.

1. Let us car-ry the sunshine wherev-er we go, It will surely make somebody glad, For a comforting word, like a clear, golden ray, Will bring help to the wea-ry and sad.
2. Let us car-ry the sunshine wherev-er we go, Let it beam from the bright, cheery face; There's a charm in the smile, there is pow'r in the glance, That betokens the heart's tender grace.
3. Let us car-ry the sunshine wherev-er we go, 'Tis the sunshine that never grows dim, When looking to Jesus, the Light of the world, We are living and shining for him.

CHORUS.

Let us car - ry the sun - shine, The beau - ti - ful, beau-ti-ful sun-shine, Let us car - ry the sun - shine, The sunshine of heaven-ly love.

carry the beau-ti-ful, beau-ti-ful sunshine, the beau - ti - ful car-ry the beauti - ful, beautiful sunshine,

Copyright, 1891, by Wm. J. Kirkpatrick.

74. Out in the Sunshine.

FANNY J. CROSBY. JNO. R. SWENEY.

1. Out in the sunshine of in-fi-nite love, Breathing the fragrance of E-den a-bove; I am so hap-py, O Sa-viour di-vine, Liv-ing or dy-ing, to know I am thine.
2. Out in the sunshine, though shadows may fall, Yet will I thank thee and praise thee for all; Nev-er, no, nev-er my heart shall re-pine, Liv-ing or dy-ing, I know I am thine.
3. Out in the sunshine sweet music I hear, Tender-ly waiting a song on my ear; Oh, what a bless-ed as-sur-ance is mine, Liv-ing or dy-ing, I know I am thine.
4. Out in the sunshine by faith I can see, Mansions in glo-ry pre-par-ing for me; O my Re-deem-er, what rap-ture is mine, Liv-ing or dy-ing, I know I am thine.

CHORUS.

Yes, . . . I am thine, . . . Lord, . . . I am thine, . . . Liv- - -ing or dy- - -ing, I know . . . I am thine.

Yes, I am thine, Lord, I am thine, Yes, I am thine, Lord, I am thine, Liv-ing or dy-ing, I know I am thine, I know, I know I am thine.

Copyright, 1891, by Jno. R. Sweney.

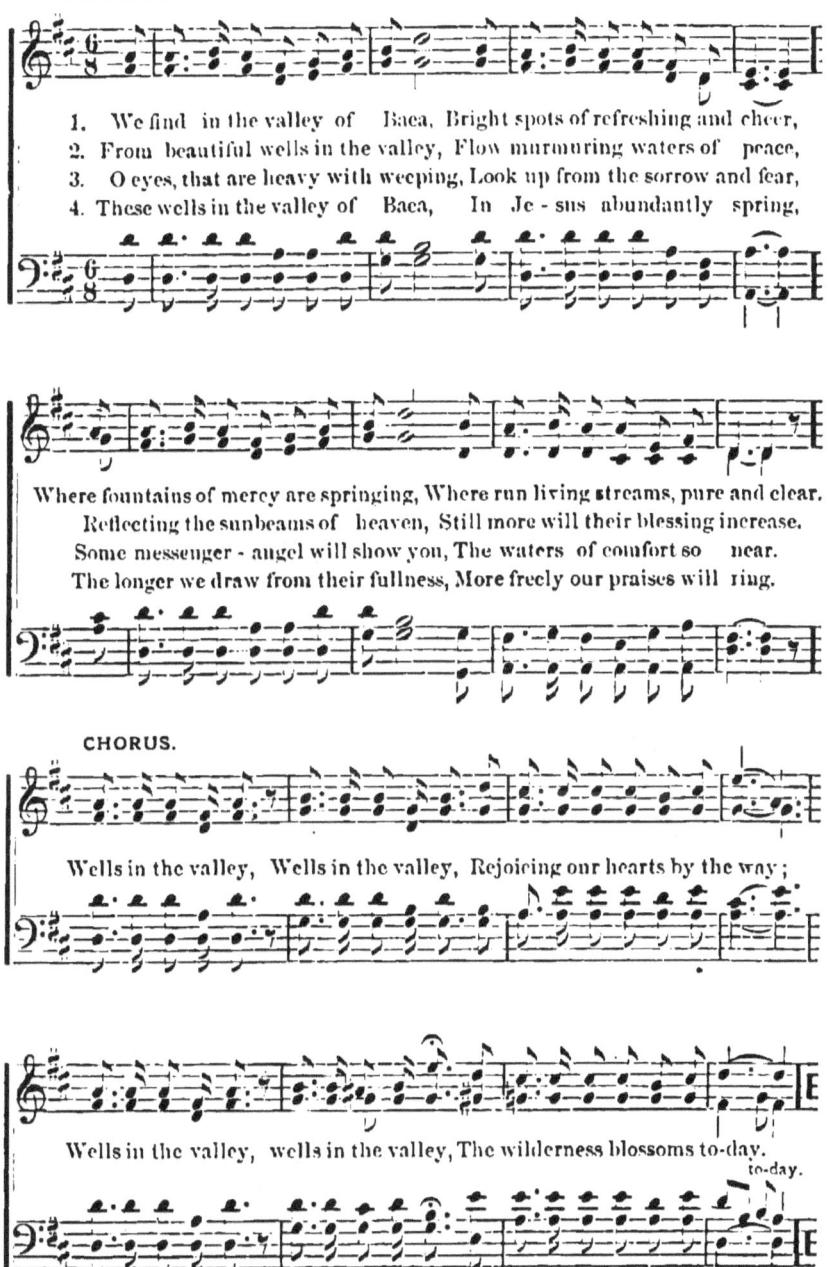

That Gentle Whisper. 81

E. E. Hewitt.   Adam Geibel.

1. Do you hear that gentle whisper? Sweeter accents cannot be;
2. Wait not till the evening shadows Close around your dark'ning way,
3. Come, and bring your fresh affections, Youth's bright flowers of joy and love,
4. Leave these shallow streams untasted, Nev - er can they sat - is - fy,

'Tis the Saviour's in - vi - ta - tion, "Come, my child, oh, come to me."
Come, while morning dew-drops sparkle, Come, while ear-ly sunbeams play.
Come, to find e - ternal treasures, Find your tru - est Friend above.
Come, to drink of living wa - ters, Freely flowing from on high.

CHORUS.

Come, oh, come; . . come, oh, come; . . Sweetly
Come, oh, come;   come, oh, come;

breathes that gentle whisper, "Come to me, oh, come to-day," Breathes the

Saviour's in - vi - ta - tion, Come to me, oh, come to-day.

Copyright, 1890, by John J. Hood.

Radiant Songs—F

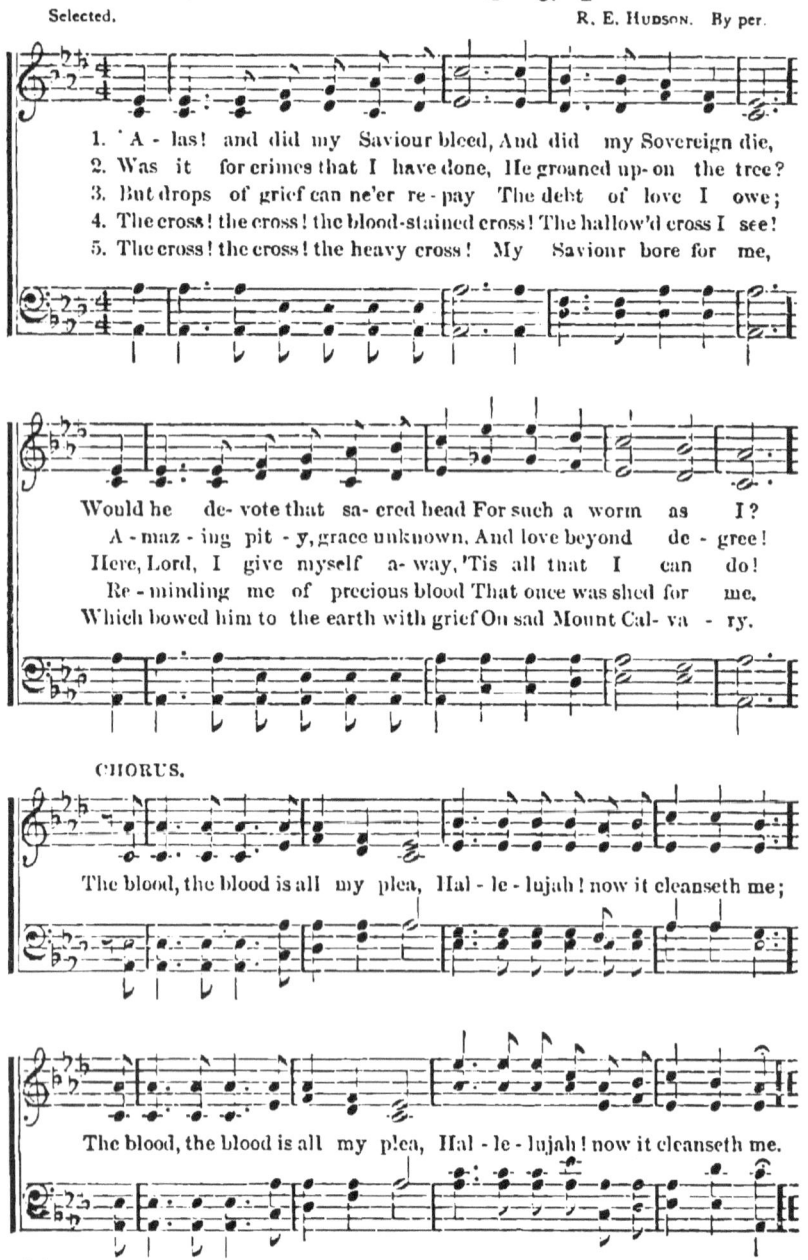

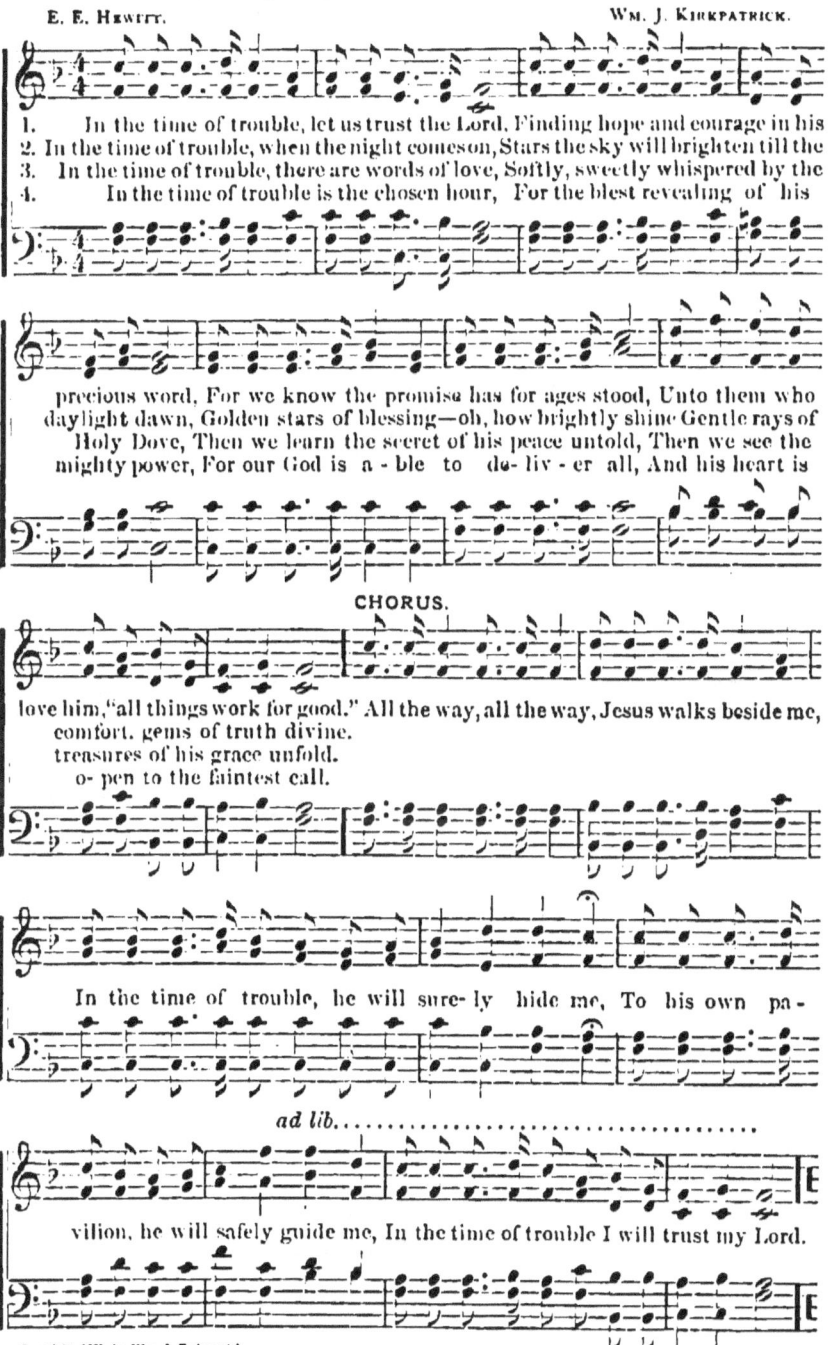

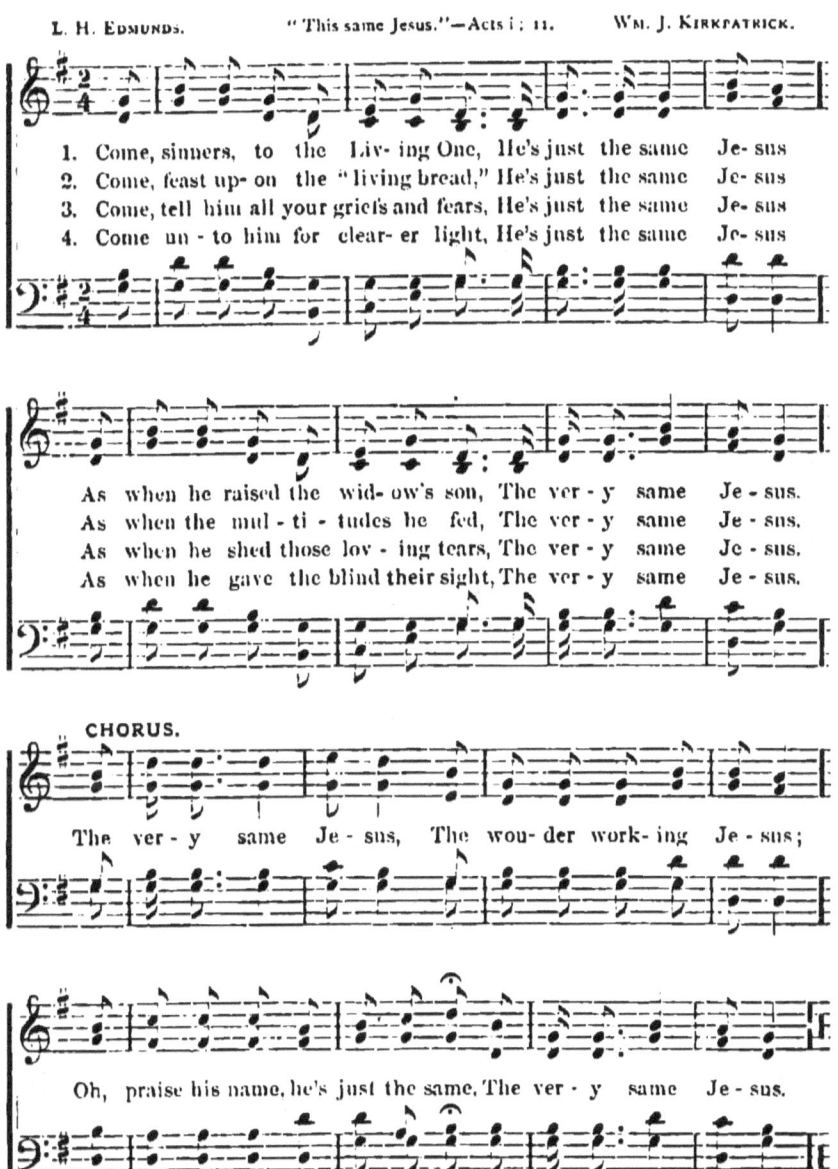

5. Calm 'midst the waves of trouble be,
　He's just the same Jesus,
　As when he hushed the raging sea,
　The very same Jesus.

6. Some day our raptured eyes shall see
　He's just the same Jesus;
　Oh, blessed day for you and me!
　The very same Jesus.

88. Is it Well with Thee?

E. E. Hewitt. 2 Kings, iv. 26. Jno. R. Sweney.

Con espress.

1. Is it well with thee? Is the buried past Beneath the crimson flow?
2. Is it well with thee? Is thy life to-day, Surrendered all to him?
3. Is it well with thee? Is thy heart at peace, Because the days to come,

Has the wounded hand swept your sins away, And made thee white as snow?
Have you learned the power of his gracious smile To chase the shadows dim?
Are ordered all by the mighty Friend, Whose love will lead thee home?

CHORUS.

For these fleeting hours, for e-ter-ni-ty, Is it well .... with thee? .... Is it well with thee?
with thee? with thee?

Copyright, 1891, by Jno. R. Sweney.

A Song of Joy. 89

"And he hath put a new song in my mouth, even praise unto our God."

H. L. G.   Psalms, xl: 3.   Dr. H. L. Gilmour.

1. The sweetest song my heart e'er sung Was one about my Lord, Of par-don free he gave to me, When I believed his word.
2. The hal-le-lu-jahs of that hour Have never passed a-way, For Christ abides, whate'er betides; My soul's a-glow to-day.
3. No harps on willow branches hang, But all in tune for God, My bounding soul, while a-ges roll, Will shout his praise a-broad.
4. No Bab-y-lo-nian rivers now, Flow by me when I weep; For tears of joy, without al-loy, Are mine while Christ doth keep.
5. Tho' trials come, and troubles too, Temptations press se-vere; My Je-sus is a conquer-or, And tells me not to fear.
6. And still the car-ol of my soul, From early morn till night, Is, "who-so-ev-er will may come," "And walk with me in white."

Oh, hal-le-lu-jah! Je-sus saves, His blood a-vails for me;

Oh, hal-le-lujah! praise the Lord, He sets his peo-ple free.

Copyright, 1889, by M. L. Gilmour.

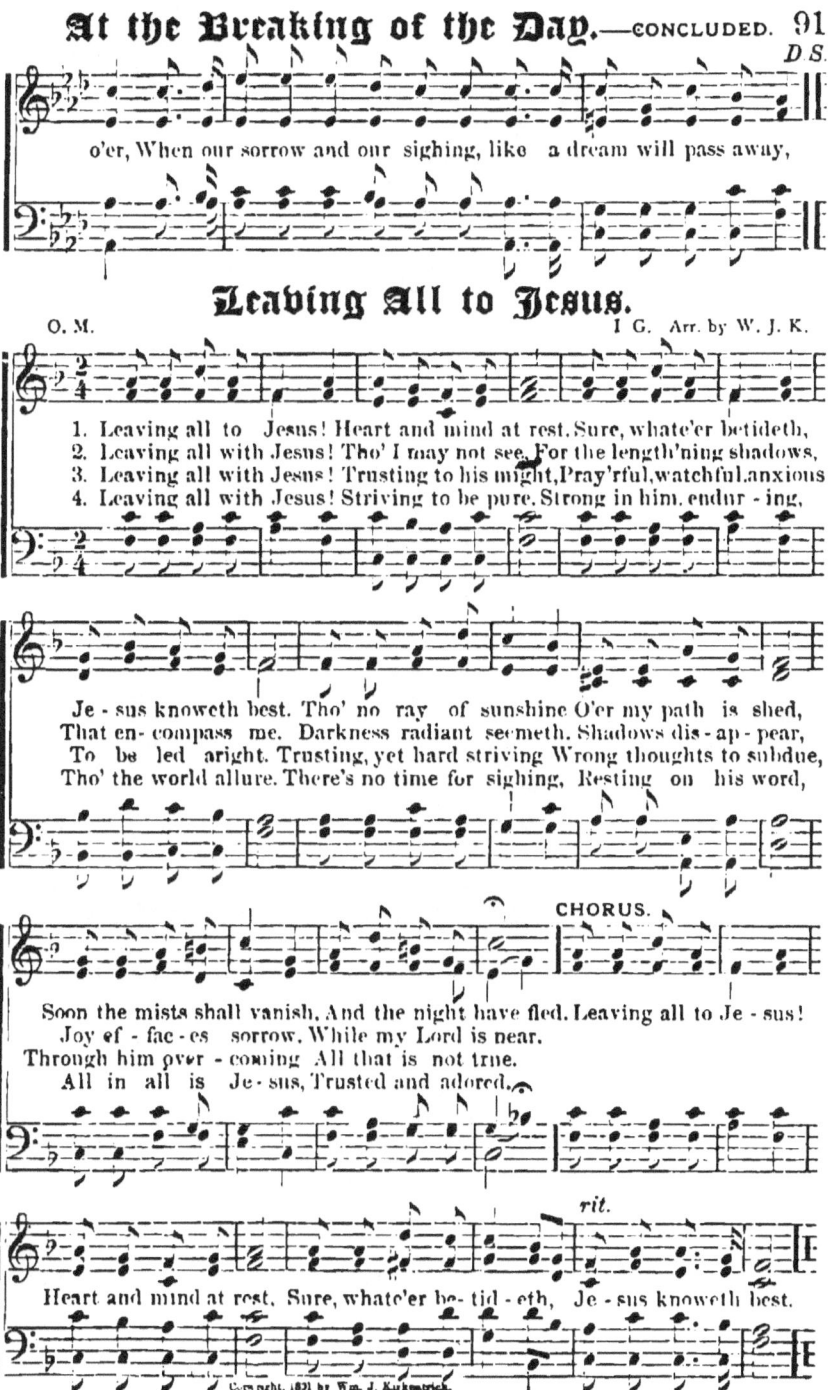

His Love Passeth Knowledge.

Fanny J. Crosby. Jno. R. Sweney.

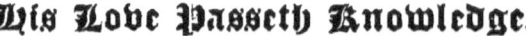

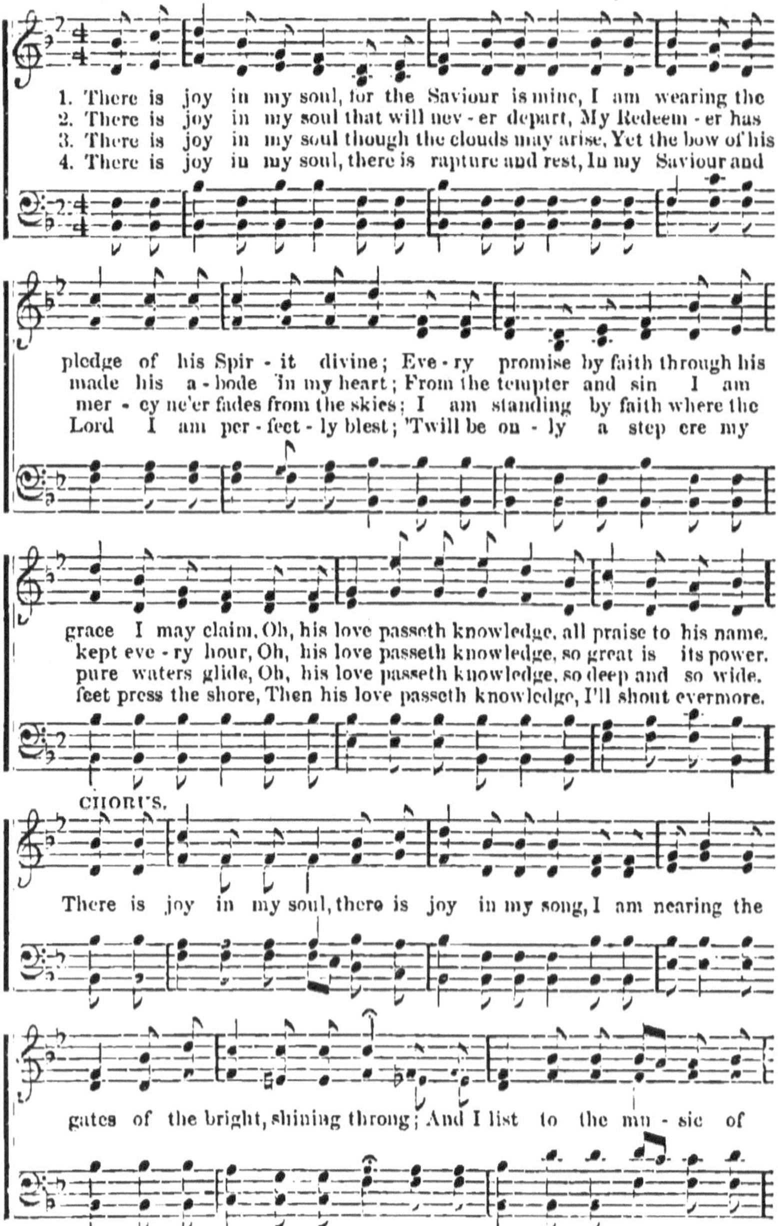

His Love Passeth.—CONCLUDED. 93

E - den so fair, Hal - le - lu - jah to Je - sus, I soon shall be there.

Save Now, O Lord. S. M.

Rev. JONATHAN DUNGAN, B. D. Wm. J. KIRKPATRICK.

1. I come with aching heart, I look, I cry to thee, For thou a gracious
2. I come with burdened soul, I anxiously implore; Make thou my broken
3. I come with bending will, I give up every sin; With thine own peace my

CHORUS.

Saviour art, Oh, come and pardon me. Save now, O Lord, I pray; Speak that
spirit whole; From sin's dark thrall restore. *Last v.*
heart now fill, And dwell thyself within. Thou hearest while I pray, Thou hast

word, forgiven; Wash the crimson stain away, Make me an heir of heaven.
all forgiven; Eve - ry stain is washed away, And I'm an heir of heaven.

4 Unworthy now I feel
  To lisp thy sacred name,
Low at thy feet I humbly kneel,
  And thy sure promise claim.

5 I know thy pardoning grace,
  I feel thy blood applied,
I see at last thy smiling face,
  My soul is satisfied.

Copyright, 1891, by Wm. J. Kirkpatrick.

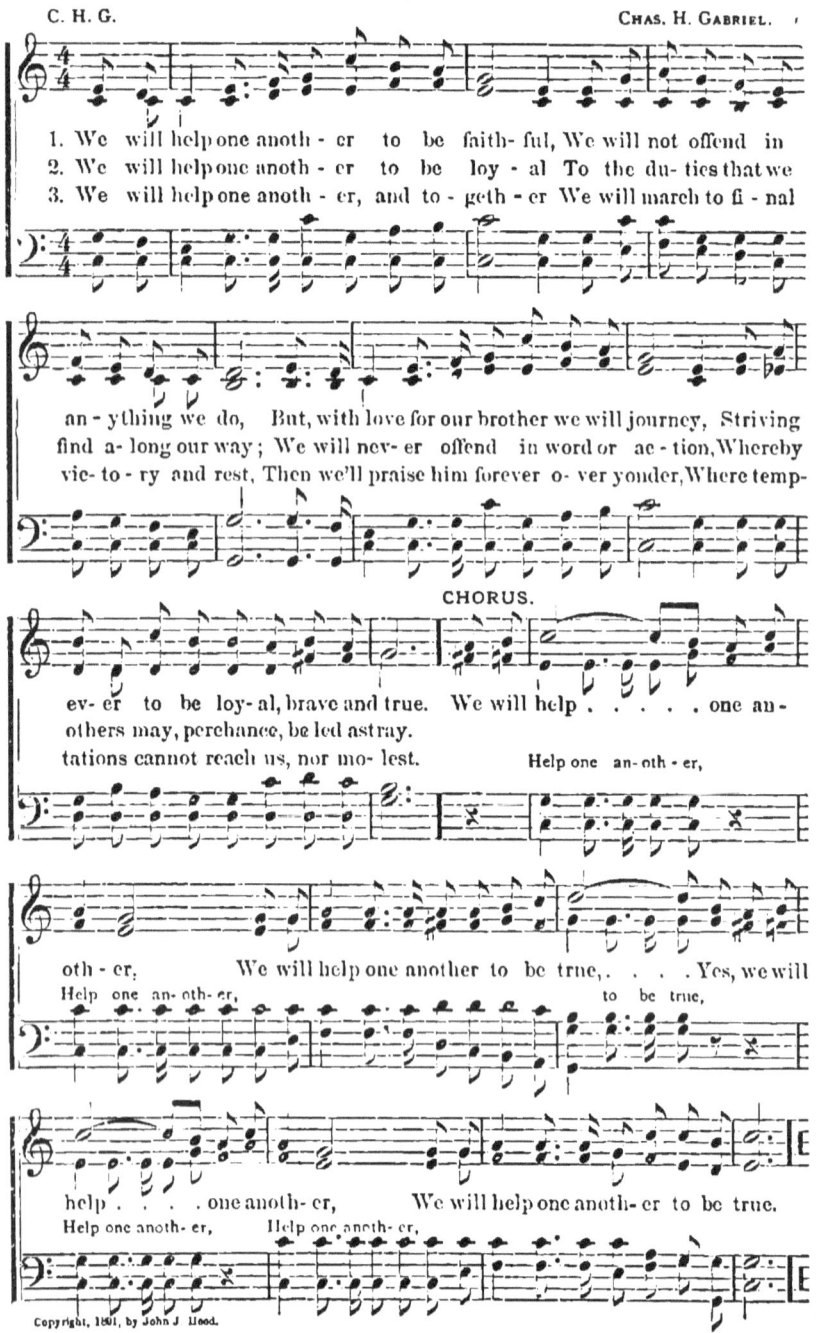

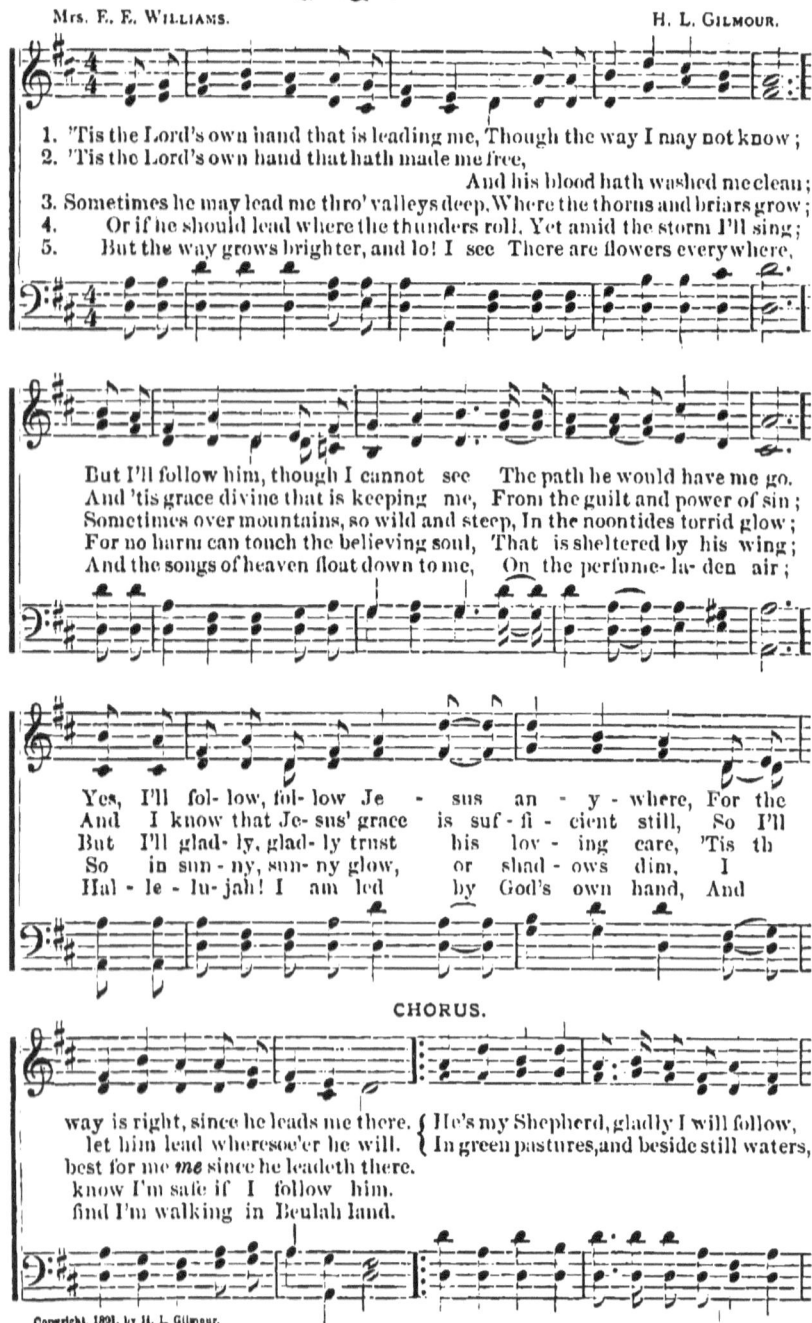

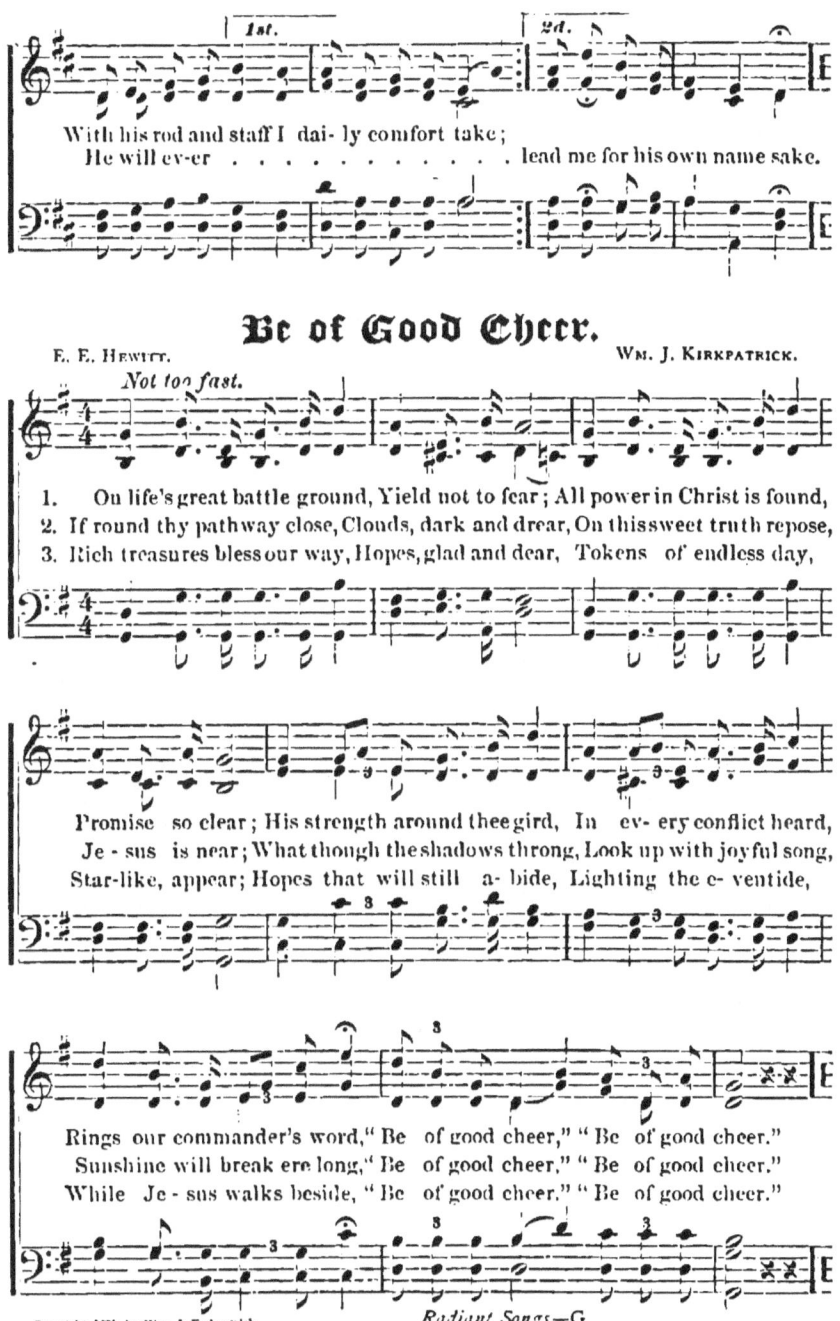

Light is Spreading.

C. H. G.   Chas. H. Gabriel.

1. Light is spreading, sing the ju-bi-lee, Shout the word from nation to
2. Light is spreading! weary one, behold! See the fruits of earnest en-
3. Light is spreading! now and evermore Trust the Lord, and herald the

na - tion! Loud the song comes ringing o'er the sea, Answering back the
deav - or,— Thir-ty, six - ty, and a hundred fold! Glory to Je - sus,
sto - ry; O - pen stands the ev - erlast- ing door, Beckoning millions

CHORUS.

joys of sal - va - tion.   Light, . . . O beautiful light . . . of
now and for - ev - er!
in - to his glo - ry.   Light, beautiful light, of   Christ and his sal-va- tion,

Christ . . . to ev - 'ry na - - - tion, Loud the song comes
Light, beautiful light of Christ to ev - 'ry na - tion,

ring- ing o'er the sea, Answering back the joys of sal - va - tion.

Copyright, 1891, by John J. Hood.

Sing, O Sing the Love.—CONCLUDED. 103

Ech - oes on . . . . the sweet re - frain.
the sweet re - frain, Ech - oes on the sweet re- frain.

Will You Rise?

MENNO B. DIEHL.   JOHN J. HOOD.

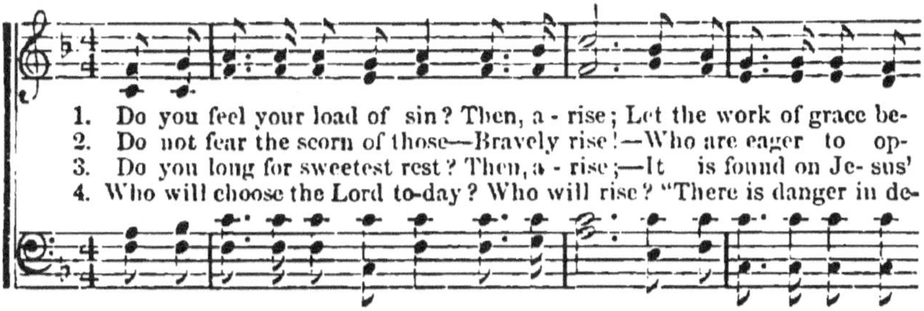

1. Do you feel your load of sin? Then, a - rise; Let the work of grace be-
2. Do not fear the scorn of those—Bravely rise!—Who are eager to op-
3. Do you long for sweetest rest? Then, a - rise;—It is found on Je- sus'
4. Who will choose the Lord to-day? Who will rise? "There is danger in de-

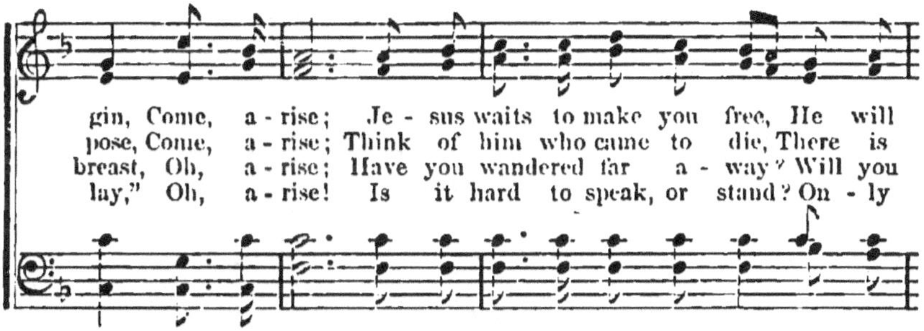

gin, Come, a - rise; Je - sus waits to make you free, He will
pose, Come, a - rise; Think of him who came to die, There is
breast, Oh, a - rise; Have you wandered far a - way? Will you
lay," Oh, a - rise! Is it hard to speak, or stand? On - ly

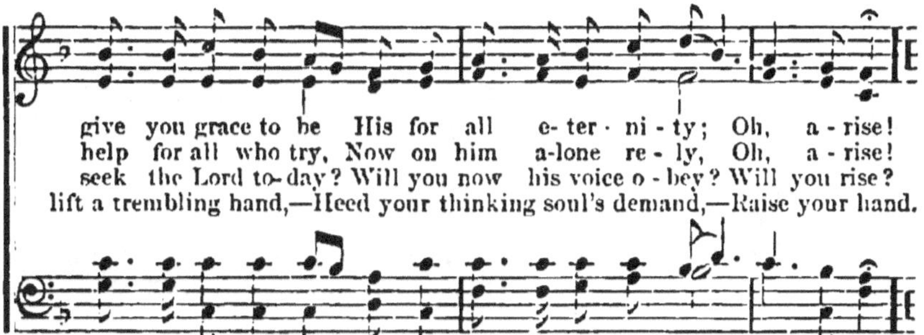

give you grace to be His for all e - ter - ni - ty; Oh, a - rise!
help for all who try, Now on him a-lone re - ly, Oh, a - rise!
seek the Lord to-day? Will you now his voice o - bey? Will you rise?
lift a trembling hand,—Heed your thinking soul's demand,—Raise your hand.

Copyright, 1891, by John J. Hood.

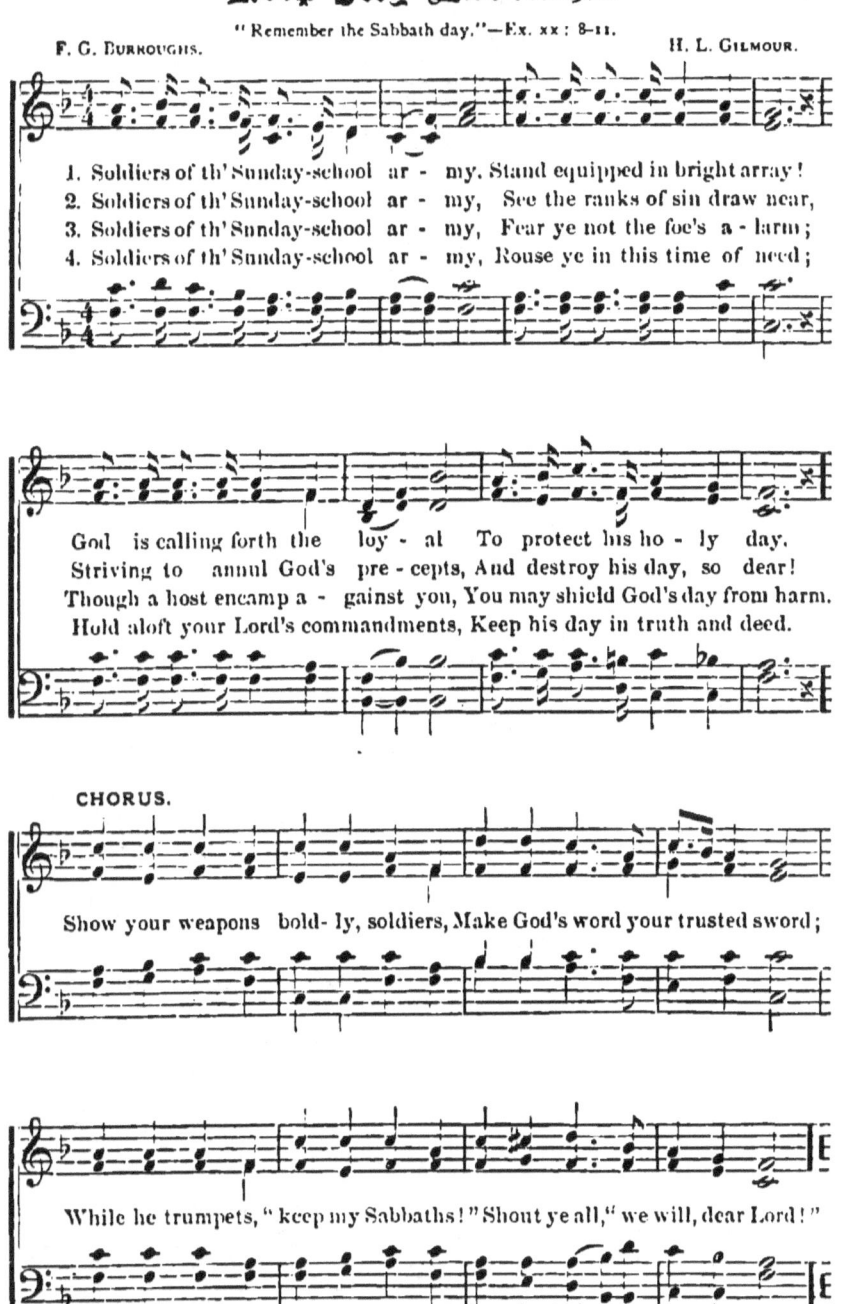

106. Going Home to Glory.

E. E. Hewitt.   Jno. R. Sweney.

1. We are go-ing home to glo-ry, we are on the shining way, On the blessed way that shineth more and more; Leading to the many mansions, brighter, brighter than the day, Where we'll meet with friends and dear ones gone before.
2. We are go-ing home to glo-ry, let us not so greatly mind If at times the road is rough that we pursue; Our best friend is close beside us, and his loving arm we'll find Strong to keep and guide us all the journey through.
3. We are go-ing home to glo-ry, O, that all the world would go! O, that all would turn and seek the "living way;" We will give the invitation, 'tis the Saviour's gentle "come," Come and seek the joys that nev-er fade away.

CHORUS.

We are go-ing home to glo-ry, we'll sing it o'er and o'er, Our Lord Je-sus, precious Je-sus, we shall see; We shall see him in his beauty,

Copyright, 1891, by Jno. R. Sweney.

Going Home to Glory.—CONCLUDED. 107

and with rapture we'll adore, Praise and serve him through a glad eternity.

For Jesus.

C. H. G.
CHAS. H. GABRIEL.

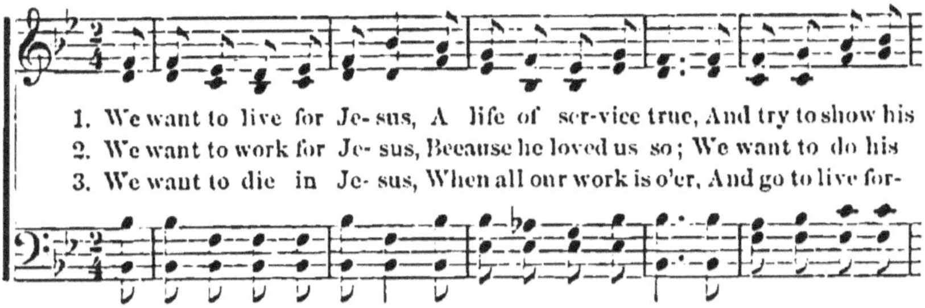

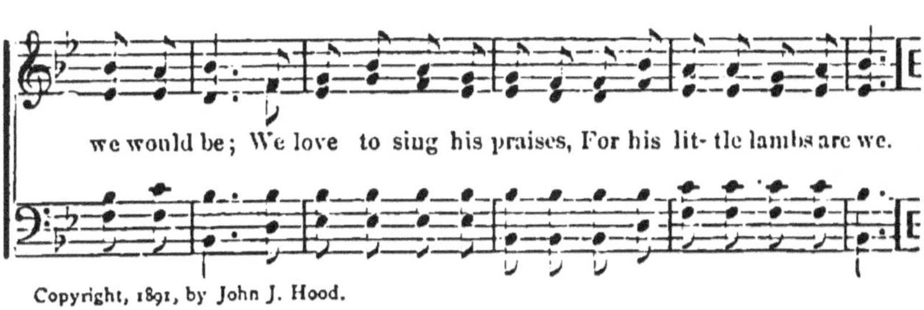

1. We want to live for Je-sus, A life of ser-vice true, And try to show his
2. We want to work for Je-sus, Because he loved us so; We want to do his
3. We want to die in Je-sus, When all our work is o'er, And go to live for-

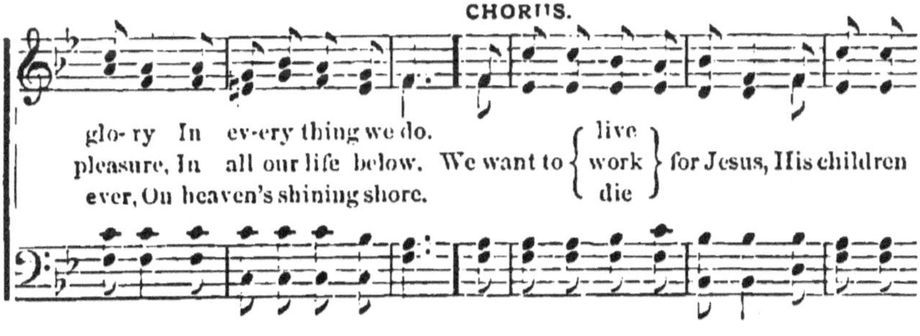

CHORUS.

glo-ry In ev-'ry thing we do.
pleasure, In all our life below. We want to { live / work / die } for Jesus, His children
ever, On heaven's shining shore.

we would be; We love to sing his praises, For his lit-tle lambs are we.

Copyright, 1891, by John J. Hood.

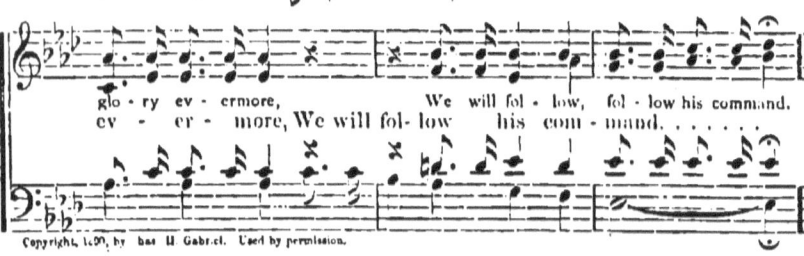

I Am Safe.—CONCLUDED. 113

tempest if his glory fills my soul, I can sing amid its raging and rejoice.

Every One may have a Friend.

E. E. Hewitt.
Jno. R. Sweney.

1. Every one may have a Friend, A loving Friend in Je - sus;
2. Every one is tru - ly blest Who finds a Friend in Je - sus;
3. Every one may have a home, Who seeks it now through Je - sus;
4. Every one may have a crown, Who bears the cross for Je - sus;

S: *Fine.*

Saving, keeping to the end, For such a Friend is Je - sus.
Love and pardon; peace and rest, We have them all in Je - sus.
To the "Father's house" he'll come, Who journeys there with Je - sus.
At his feet to lay it down, And glo - ry give to Je - sus.

D. S.—Every one a Friend may win, A loving Friend in Je - sus.

CHORUS. *D.S.*

Every one who turns from sin, Asks the blessed Saviour in,

Copyright, 1891, by Jno. R. Sweney.

Radiant Songs—H

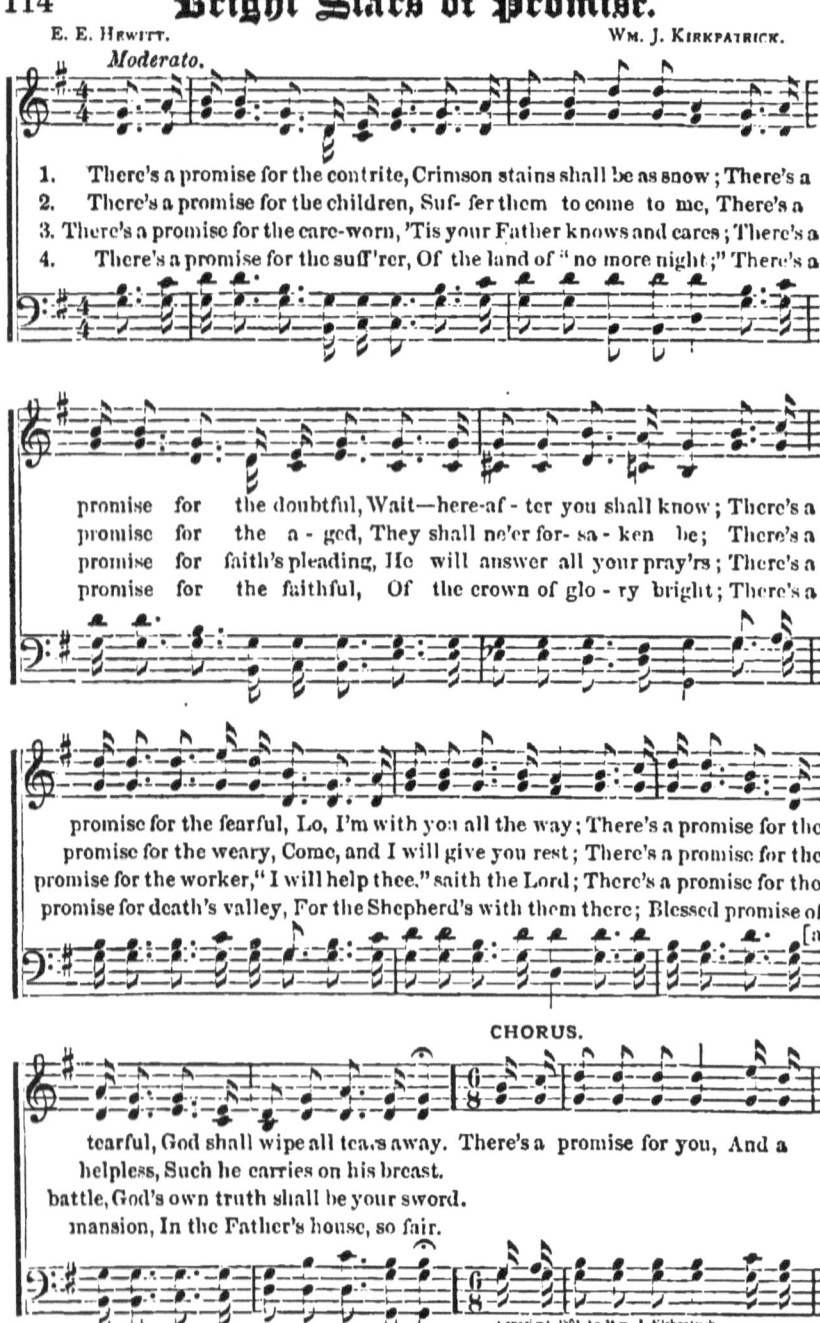

The Wondrous Love of Jesus.

Lizzie Edwards. Jno. R. Sweney.

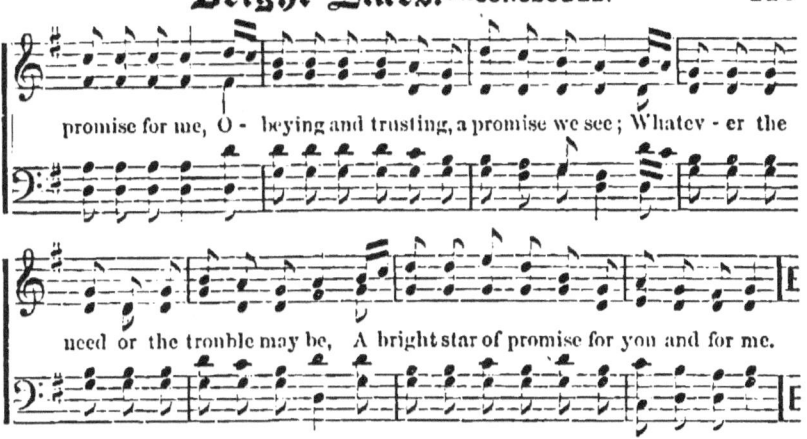

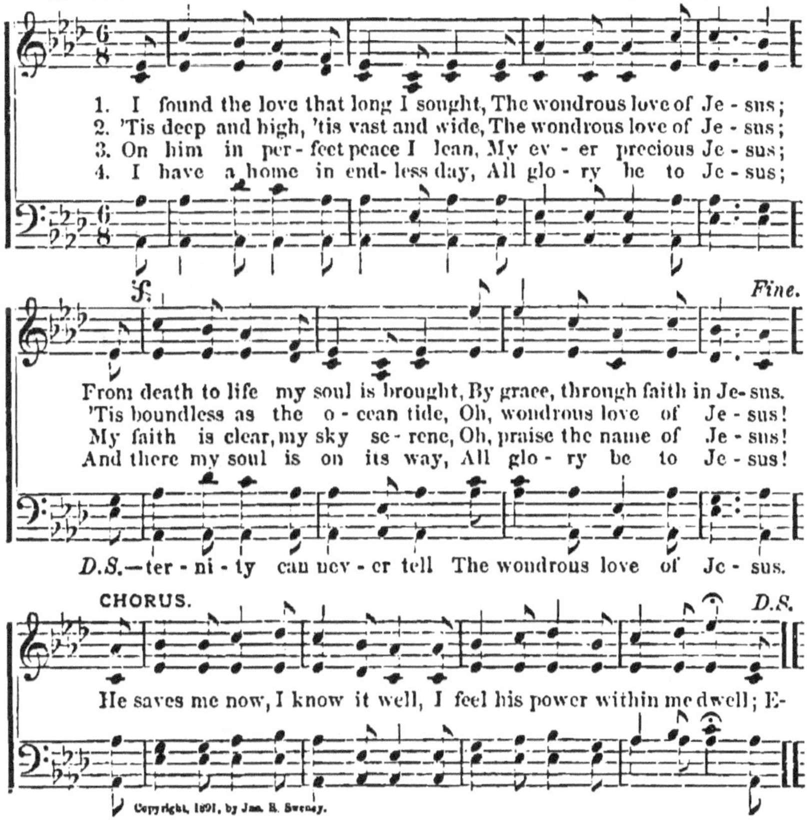

Not One Thing hath Failed Us. 117

E. E. Hewitt.
Jno. R. Sweney.

1. Not one thing hath failed us Of his word of grace; Gratefully the blessings
2. Every golden promise, When we sought its light, With an undimmed lustre
3. Heeding the Good Shepherd, Oft he brought our feet To the richest pastures,
4. Need we dread the future, Trusting in his name? Through the years before us

Of the past we trace; For our dai-ly hunger Dai-ly manna fell;
Sparkled clear and bright; Ev-ery night of weeping Brought a rosy dawn,
Sunny, fresh and sweet; When his guidance led us Thro' some gloomy vale
He is still "the same." We will sing in glory,'Round the "sea of glass,"

CHORUS.

In the wea-ry des-ert Sprang the living well. Not . . . one thing hath
When new songs of gladness Hailed the glowing morn.
He was there beside us, Love can nev-er fail.
"Not one thing hath failed us," "All are come to pass." Not one thing hath failed us,

failed us Of . . . . his word of grace; . . . .
Not one thing hath failed us Of his word of grace, Of his word of grace;

Grate - - fully the bless - - ings Of the past we trace.
Gratefully the bless - ings, Gratefully the blessings

Copyright, 1891, by John R. Sweney.

118. Hold Out the Hand.

LANTA WILSON SMITH. WM. J. KIRKPATRICK.

1. You've read what our Lord in his pilgrimage here
Bestowed by the touch of his hand,
2. The little ones came, and the sinful and sad Were won by his kind, tender way;
Rich blessing, full pardon, and healing divine,
E'en storms knew his wave of command.
Just try what the touch of a true, loving hand Will do for the wand'rers to-day.

CHORUS.
Then hold out the hand, hold out the hand, To-day 'tis the world's great demand,
All around you are brothers who waitingly stand, Then hold out, hold out the hand.

3 There's something divine in the clasp of the hand,
There's-a power beyond what we [know;
And the sorrowing world has a right to demand,
That the Christian should sympathy [show.

4 Reach out for the brother that's drifting away,
From out the safe harbor of right,
Don't shun him, or treat him with self-righteous scorn,
A hand-shake may save him to-night.

5 The old, the forsaken, the sorrowing ones,
How great are the burdens they bear;
Kind actions and words will bring comfort and cheer,
And save from the blight of despair.

6 Great deeds are performed by the chosen and few,
While dreamers in idleness stand;
Slight actions have sometimes the graudest results,
Then prayerfully hold out your hand.

Copyright, 1891, by Wm. J. Kirkpatrick.

Falter Not.

FANNY J. CROSBY. JNO. R. SWENEY.

1. Fal-ter not nor look behind thee, Cast thy ev-ery weight aside,
2. Fal-ter not nor look behind thee, Firm and fearless take thy place,
3. Fal-ter not nor look behind thee, Lest thy la-bor prove in vain;
4. Fal-ter not nor look behind thee, Lo, the prize is just in sight,
5. Fal-ter not nor look behind thee, What of all thy tri-als past,

Haste to win the prize before thee, Trusting him, thy Precious Guide.
Robe and crown and palm are wait'ng For the vic-tors in the race.
Run with pa-tience, and remember Thou hast much to lose or gain.
One more struggle, meet it bravely, Speed thee on with all thy might.
If by grace through faith in Jesus, Thine the vic-tor's crown at last?

CHORUS.

Fal-ter not . . . . nor look be-hind thee, Still thy
Fal-ter not nor look be- - -hind thee,

course . . . . with joy pur-sue; . . . . Per-se-vere, ... for
Still thy course with joy pur-sue; Per-se-vere, for thou

thou must con-quer, With the cross . . . . of Christ in view. . . . .
must con- quer, With the cross of Christ in view.

Copyright, 1891, by Jno. R. Sweney.

126. Come to the Cross.

SALLIE MARTIN.   JNO. R. SWENEY.

1. Come to the cross, thy Redeem-er is there, On-ly a look, and a pen-i-tent prayer; On-ly be-lieve, and thy soul shall be free,
2. Come un-to him, and be cleansed in his blood, Plunged in the depths of the life-giv-ing flood; Je-sus is wait-ing his mer-cy to show,
3. Come to the feast of the gos-pel to-day, All things are ready, then where-fore de-lay? Grieve not the Spir-it, oh, slight him no more;
4. Come to the fold and the Shepherd so dear, Now to receive thee, be-hold, he is near; Blest and for-ev-er with him thou canst be,—

CHORUS.

Je-sus is waiting, O lost one, for thee. Come, come, come, just as thou art, Come, come, come, give him thy heart; On-ly believe, and thy soul shall be free, Je-sus is waiting, O lost one, for thee.

Wait-ing to make thee as pure as the snow.
Haste, or thy sea-son of grace will be o'er.
Still he is watching and wait-ing for thee.

Copyright, 1891, by Jno. R. Sweney.

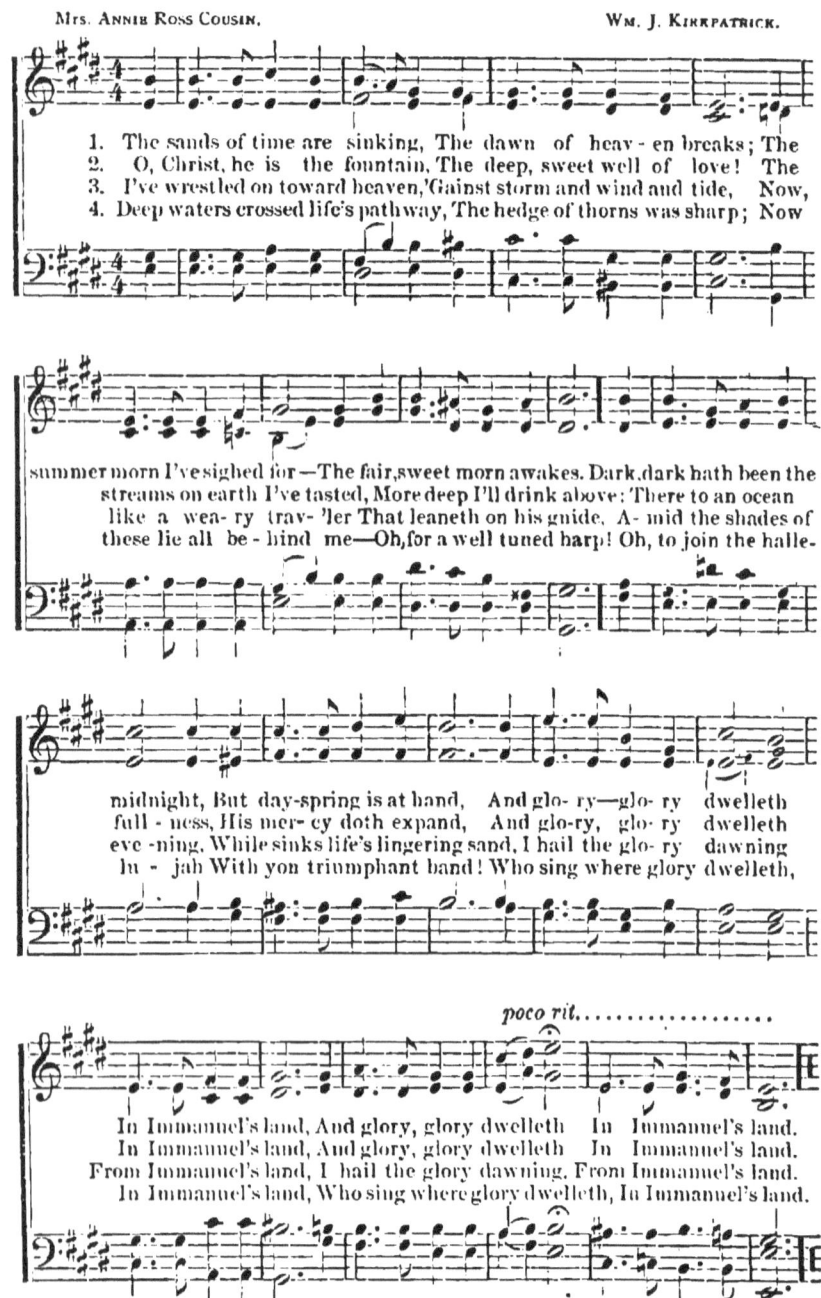

5 Nay, I would this proffered hand take,
  Knowing that it leads aright;
  Yes, I would this loving choice make;
  Trusting in his love and might.

6 Then, as hand in hand together
  With my Saviour with my Friend,
  With my Christ, my Elder Brother,
  Let him lead till life shall end.

Rescue Them. 137

L. H. Edmunds.   Wm. J. Kirkpatrick.

1. Christian, to the rescue! Hasten souls to save; Lis-ten to the warning,
2. Tar-ry not, nor fal-ter, Souls are in distress; Ea-ger, glad to help them,
3. While the toilers bravely Seek the tempest-tossed, Thro' the dashing breakers,
4. Here's the mighty Captain Standing by our side, Faith, and strength, and courage

Sounding o'er the wave; See the signals fly-ing From the sinking ship;
Who will answer "yes"? Read-y now the life-boat, Be it nobly manned;
Lest a soul be lost,—All who lift pe-ti-tions Shall their labors share,
Free-ly he'll pro-vide; Now a ray of glo-ry Breaks the shadows dim;

CHORUS.

Let the cry for helpers Pass from lip to lip.   Rescue them, rescue them;
Earnest, faithful workers, Christ's own loyal band.
Thro' the lonely night-watch Prevalent in prayer.
Present, sure salva-tion, Trusting all to him.

Who will volunteer? In the name of Jesus haste to save and cheer; Rescue them,

rescue them, Christian volunteer,
         Strangers, friends, or brothers, Haste to save and cheer.

Copyright, 1901, by Wm J Kirkpatrick

Work for the Master.—CONCLUDED. 139

something for Je- sus! The Master is call - ing, O serve him to - day.

When shall We all Meet again?

Arr. by L. H. EDMUNDS. Adapted and arr. by WM. J. KIRKPATRICK.

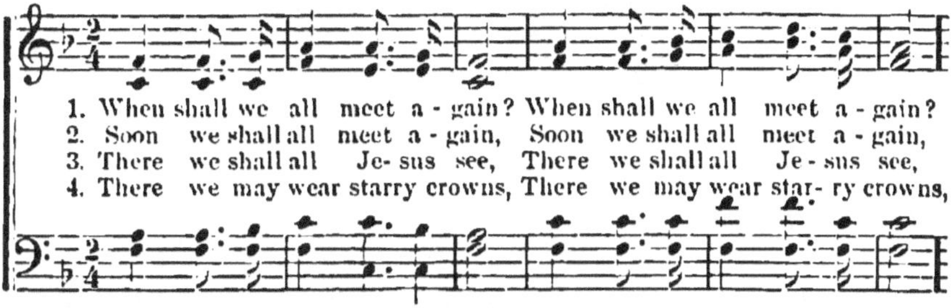

1. When shall we all meet a - gain? When shall we all meet a - gain?
2. Soon we shall all meet a - gain, Soon we shall all meet a - gain,
3. There we shall all Je- sus see, There we shall all Je - sus see,
4. There we may wear starry crowns, There we may wear star- ry crowns,

When shall we all meet a - gain? If not on earth, in heav- en
Soon we shall all meet a - gain, If not on earth, in heav- en
There we shall all Je- sus see, If not on earth, in heav- en
There we may wear starry crowns. Tho' not on earth, in heav- en

Shall we all meet a - gain?
We shall all meet a - gain.
We shall all Je - sus see.
We may all wear bright crowns.

5 ‖: There we shall meet friends we love, :‖
When we get home to heaven
We shall meet friends we love.

6 ‖: There we shall *never* part again, :‖
When we get home to heaven
We shall *never* part again.

7 ‖: There we shall *never* say good-by, :‖
When we get home to heaven
We shall *never* say good-by.

Copyright, 1891, by Wm. J. Kirkpatrick.

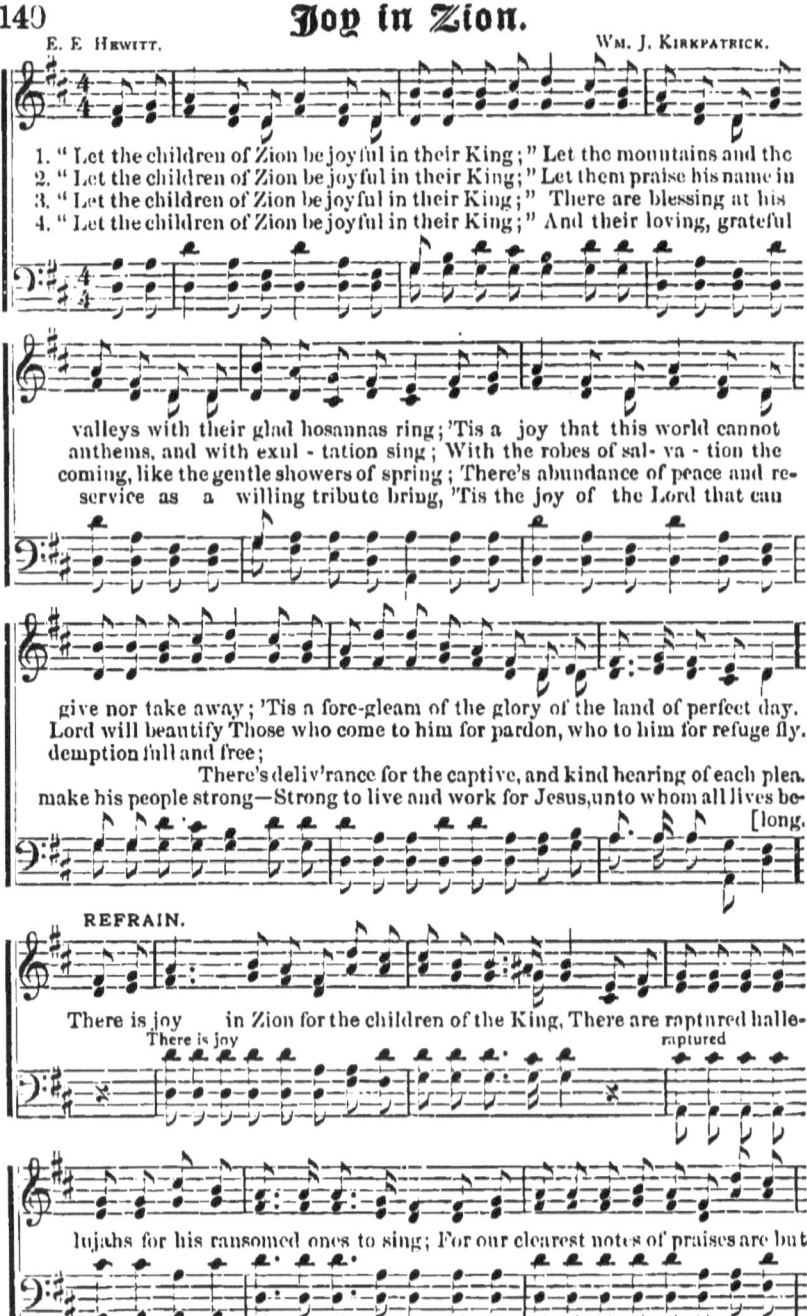

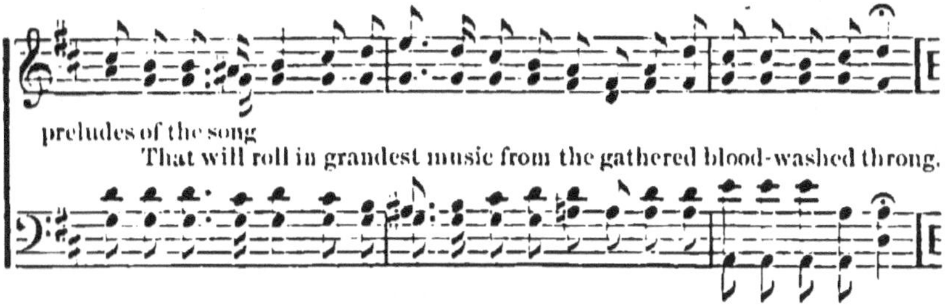

Joy in Zion.—CONCLUDED. 141

preludes of the song
That will roll in grandest music from the gathered blood-washed throng.

O Precious Jesus.

Rev. Robt. Pierce.   1 Peter ii: 7.   H. L. Gilmour.

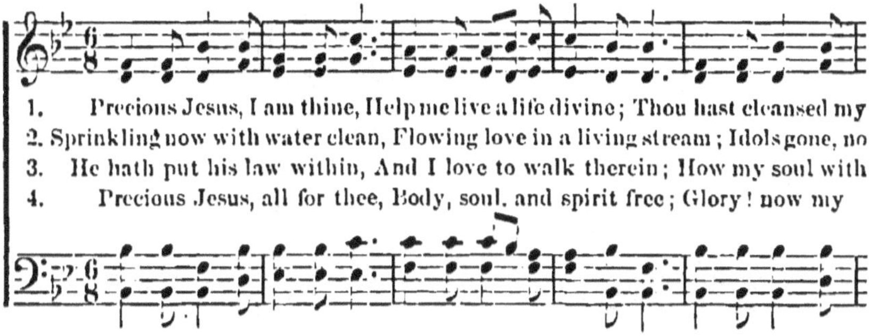

1. Precious Jesus, I am thine, Help me live a life divine; Thou hast cleansed my
2. Sprinkling now with water clean, Flowing love in a living stream; Idols gone, no
3. He hath put his law within, And I love to walk therein; How my soul with
4. Precious Jesus, all for thee, Body, soul, and spirit free; Glory! now my

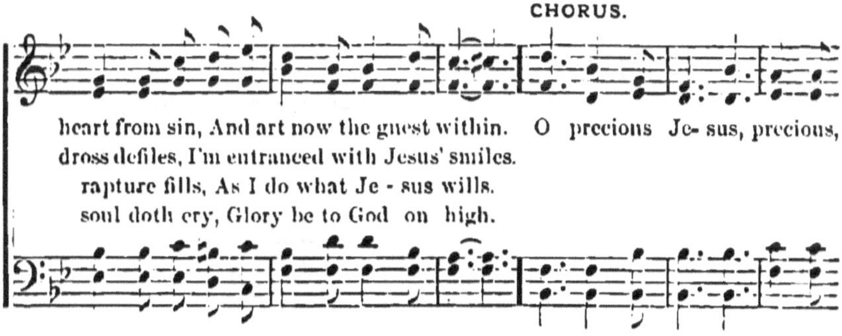

CHORUS.

heart from sin, And art now the guest within.   O precious Je- sus, precious,
dross defiles, I'm entranced with Jesus' smiles.
rapture fills, As I do what Je - sus wills.
soul doth cry, Glory be to God on high.

precious Jesus, Precious now to my glad soul, For thy blood hath made me whole.

Copyright, 1891, by H. L. Gilmour.

144. O Blessed Way.

Fanny J. Crosby.   Jno. R. Sweney.

1. Thou art, O Lord, the Truth, the Life, And thro' this world of toil and strife
2. Thou art the Vine, the branches we, And if our souls a-bide in thee
3. Thou art our Rock of A-ges past, The Rock that shall for-ev-er last;
4. Thou art the Light that cheers our gloom, And guides us safe beyond the tomb;

Thou art the Way, by whom alone Our pray'rs can reach thy gracious throne.
No ill can harm, nor fear de-stroy Our peaceful rest, our ho-ly joy.
Thou art the Word that can-not fail, Though all the hosts of death as-sail.
Thou art our King, to whom is given All power on earth and all in heaven.

CHORUS.

O blessed Way, ... O Truth di-vine, ... O
    O bless-ed Way,   O Truth di-vine,

Life where endless glories ever shine; . . . Hide thou our lives . . . . Till we shall
    ev-er shine,   Hide thou our lives

wake, ... And in-to ho-ly songs of rapture break. . . .
till we shall wake,   rapture break.

Copyright, 1891, by Jno. R. Sweney.

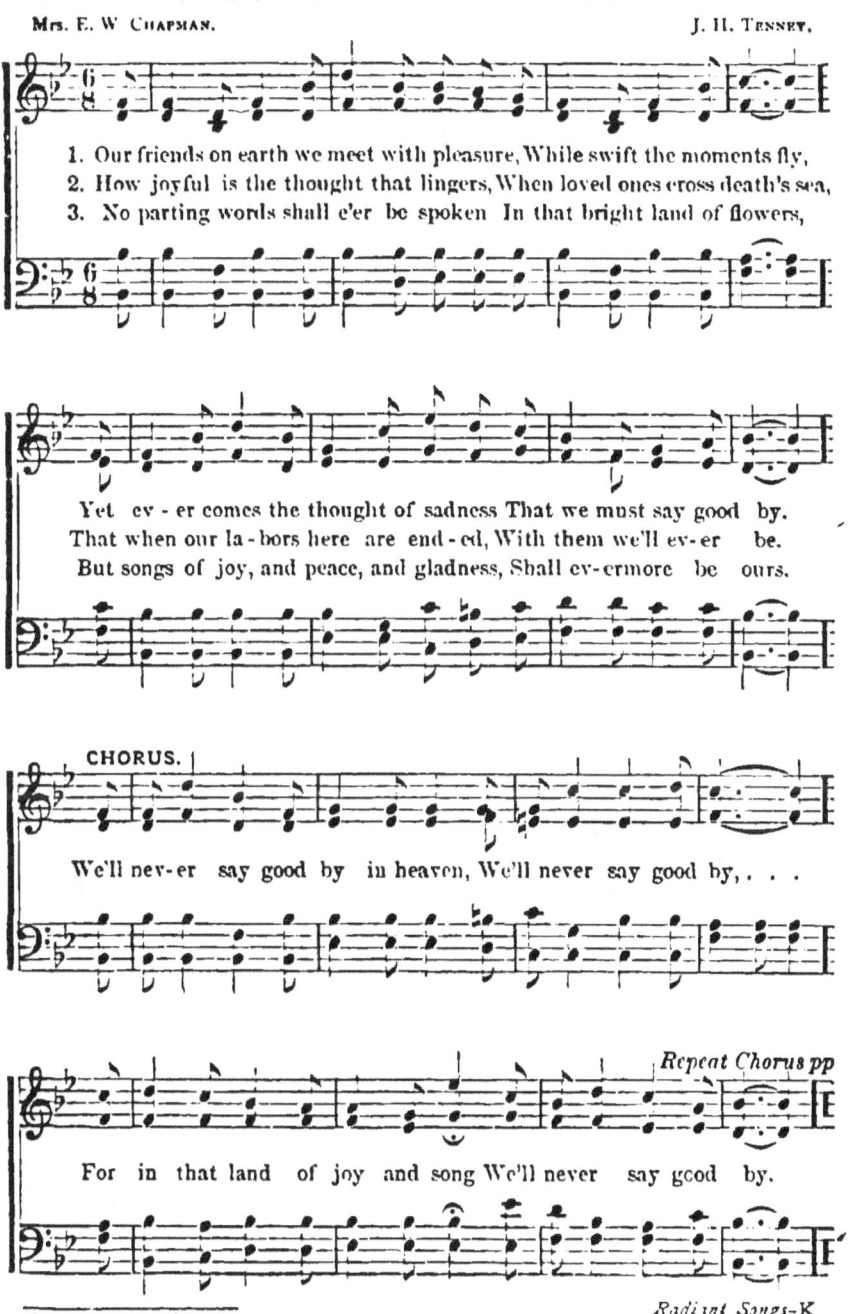

The Gospel Bells.—CONCLUDED.

Lead Me, Ever Lead Me.

IDA. L. REED.   JNO. R. SWENEY.

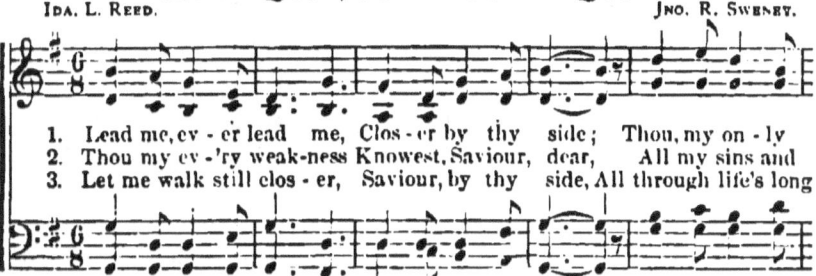

1. Lead me, ev - er lead me, Clos - er by thy side; Thou, my on - ly
2. Thou my ev - 'ry weak-ness Knowest, Saviour, dear, All my sins and
3. Let me walk still clos - er, Saviour, by thy side, All through life's long

Cho.—Lead me, ev - er lead me, Hold my hand in thine, Keep me ev - er

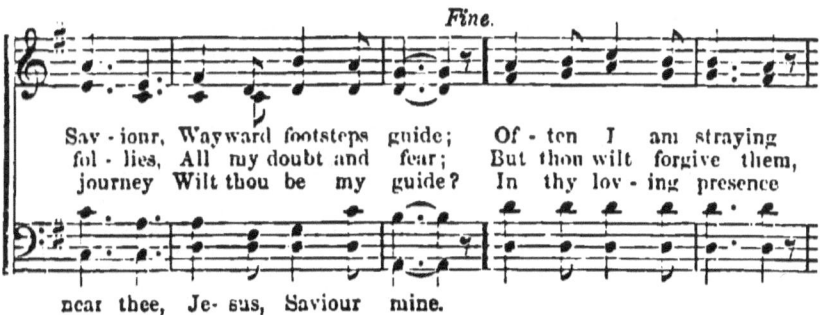

Fine.

Sav - iour, Wayward footsteps guide; Of - ten I am straying
fol - lies, All my doubt and fear; But thou wilt forgive them,
journey Wilt thou be my guide? In thy lov - ing presence

near thee, Je- sus, Saviour mine.

Chorus, D C

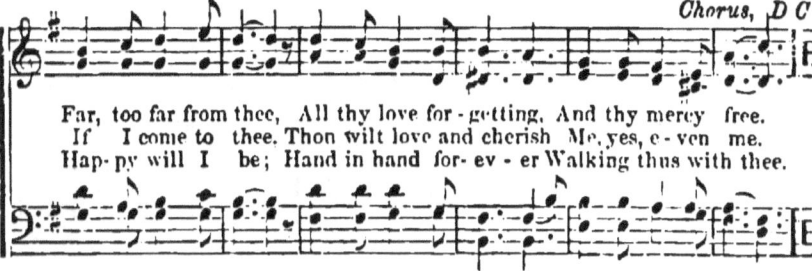

Far, too far from thee, All thy love for - getting, And thy mercy free.
If I come to thee, Thou wilt love and cherish Me, yes, e - ven me.
Hap - py will I be; Hand in hand for - ev - er Walking thus with thee.

Copyright, 1891, by John R. Sweney.

It is Time to Seek.—CONCLUDED. 149

loosed the "silver cord," Even now, even now! Even now, even now! It is time to seek the Lord.

Jesus is Calling.

F. A. B.   F. A. BLACKMER. Chorus arr.

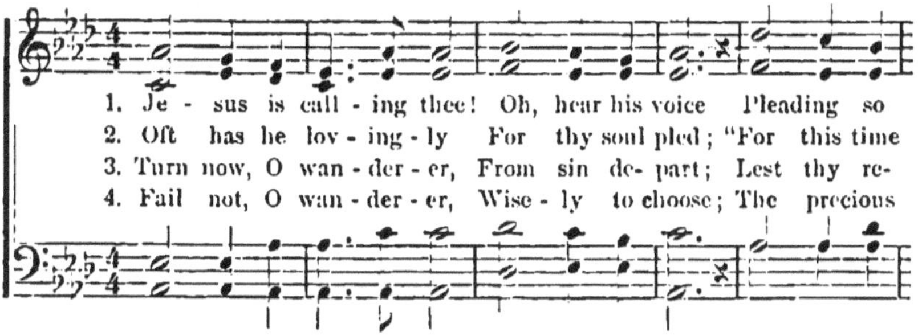

1. Je - sus is call - ing thee! Oh, hear his voice Pleading so
2. Oft has he lov - ing - ly For thy soul pled; "For this time
3. Turn now, O wan - der - er, From sin de - part; Lest thy re-
4. Fail not, O wan - der - er, Wise - ly to choose; The precious

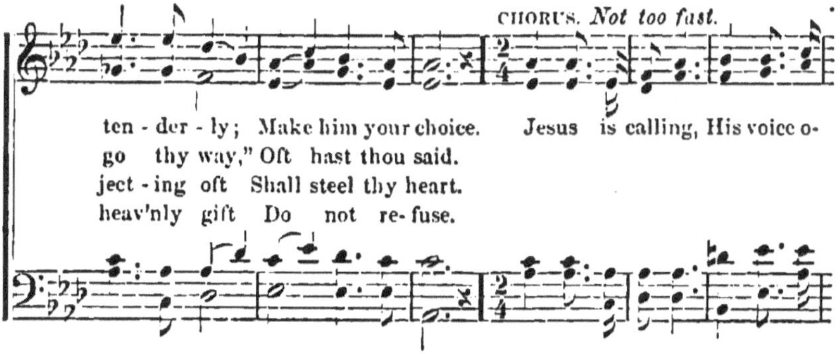

CHORUS. *Not too fast.*

ten - der - ly; Make him your choice.
go thy way," Oft hast thou said.
ject - ing oft Shall steel thy heart.
heav'nly gift Do not re - fuse.

Jesus is calling, His voice o-bey; Child, come home, No longer roam, O sinner, come to-day.

Copyright, 1881, by John J. Hood.

150. Where Do You Journey?

"We are journeying unto the place of which the Lord said, I will give it you." Num. x. 29.

F. G. Burroughs.   H. L. Gilmour.

Question.

1. Whither do you journey, sail-or, O'er the o-cean deep and wide?
2. What if tempests rock thy ves-sel, And the an-gry waves dash high?
3. When the darkness gathers 'round you, And you see no lighthouse ray

Do you seek a bet-ter country, Far beyond this swelling tide?
What if per-ils throug a-bout thee,—Unseen dangers hov-er nigh?
Gleam a-cross the troubled waters, Sail-or, will you know the way?

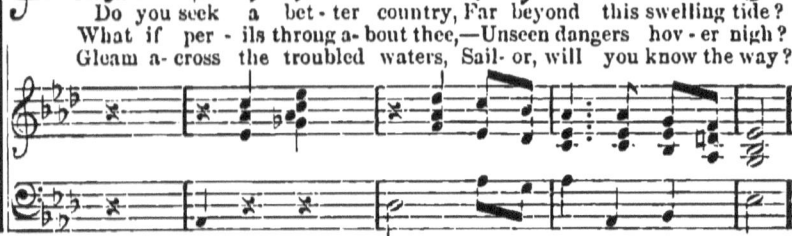

Response.

Yes, it is the land of Canaan, Where my heart and treasures are;
Christ will be my faithful Pi-lot, On his grace I can depend;
Bethlehem's Star can nev-er fail me, Lo, its blessed, golden light

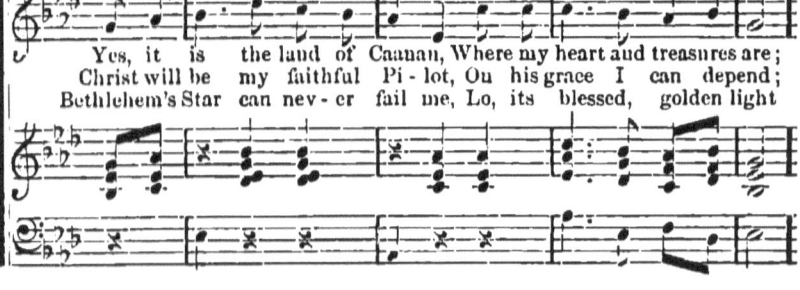

'Tis a land of milk and honey; And the journey is not far.
Safely on shall glide my vessel, E-ven to my journey's end.
Guides me onward toward that cit-y, Where there are no tears, no night.

Copyright, 1891, by H. L. Gilmour.

154. I Will Shout His Praise in Glory.

P. H. Dingman.   Jno. R. Sweney.

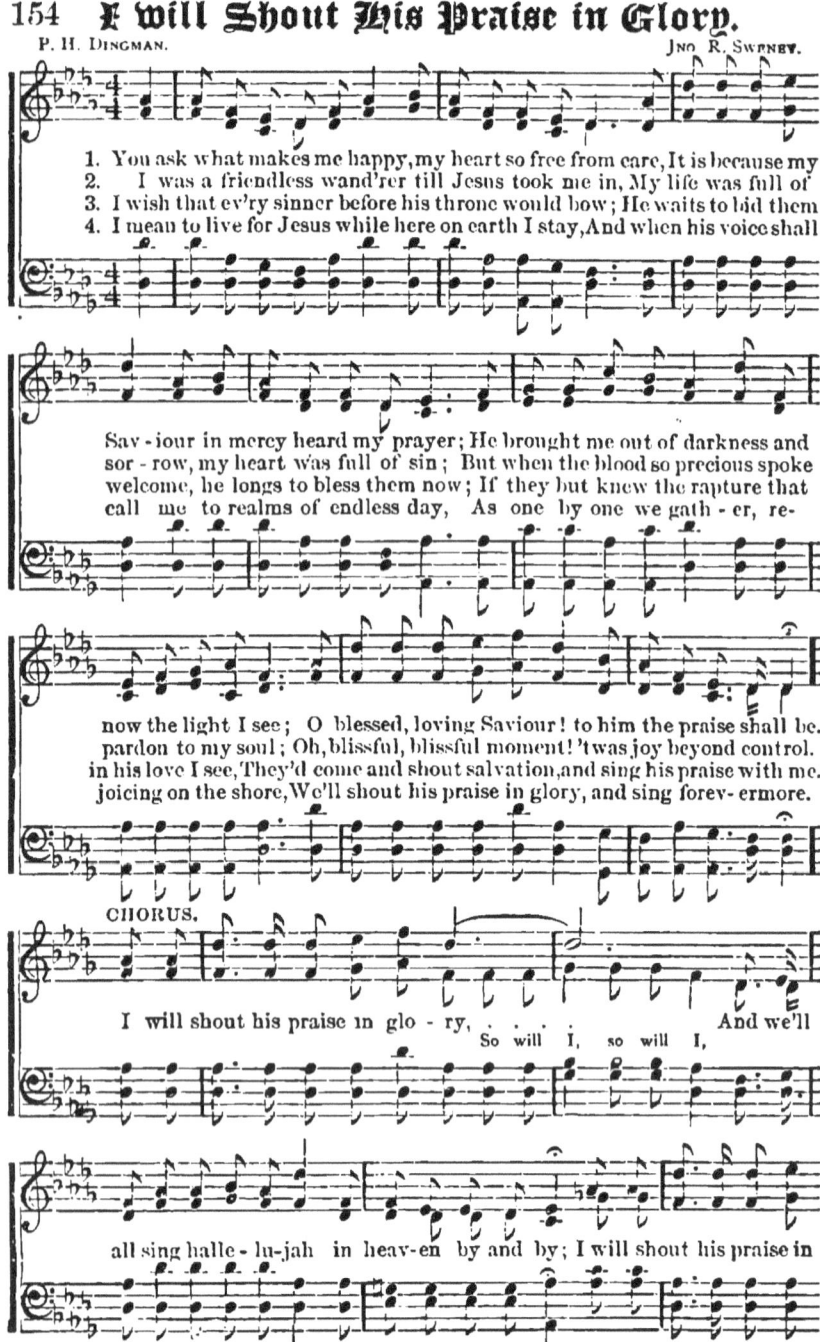

1. You ask what makes me happy, my heart so free from care, It is because my
2. I was a friendless wand'rer till Jesus took me in, My life was full of
3. I wish that ev'ry sinner before his throne would bow; He waits to bid them
4. I mean to live for Jesus while here on earth I stay, And when his voice shall

Sav-iour in mercy heard my prayer; He brought me out of darkness and
sor-row, my heart was full of sin; But when the blood so precious spoke
welcome, he longs to bless them now; If they but knew the rapture that
call me to realms of endless day, As one by one we gath-er, re-

now the light I see; O blessed, loving Saviour! to him the praise shall be.
pardon to my soul; Oh, blissful, blissful moment! 'twas joy beyond control.
in his love I see, They'd come and shout salvation, and sing his praise with me.
joicing on the shore, We'll shout his praise in glory, and sing forev-ermore.

CHORUS.

I will shout his praise in glo - ry, ... And we'll
So will I, so will I,

all sing halle-lu-jah in heav-en by and by; I will shout his praise in

Copyright, 1889, by Jno. R. Sweney.

Beautiful Robes.—CONCLUDED. 157

Gar - - ments of light, ... Love - - ly and bright, . . .
Garments of light, . . Garments of light, Lovely and bright, . . Lovely and bright,

Walking with Jesus in white, Beau-ti-ful robes we shall wear.

The Golden Key.

"Prayer is the key to unlock the door, and the bolt to shut in the night."

JNO. R. SWENEY.

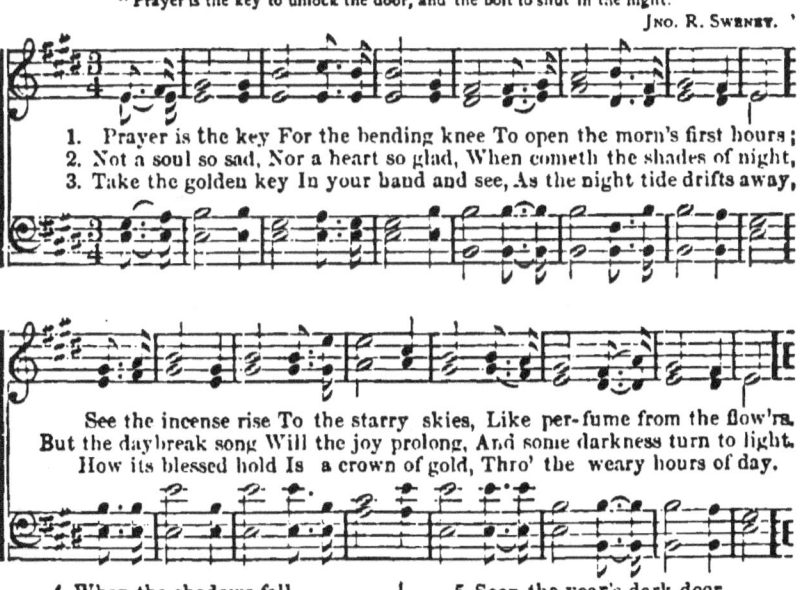

1. Prayer is the key For the bending knee To open the morn's first hours;
2. Not a soul so sad, Nor a heart so glad, When cometh the shades of night,
3. Take the golden key In your hand and see, As the night tide drifts away,

See the incense rise To the starry skies, Like per-fume from the flow'rs.
But the daybreak song Will the joy prolong, And some darkness turn to light.
How its blessed hold Is a crown of gold, Thro' the weary hours of day.

4 When the shadows fall,
And the vesper call
Is sobbing its low refrain,
'Tis a garland sweet
To the toil dent feet,
And an antidote for pain

5 Soon the year's dark door
Shall be shut no more:
Life's tears shall be wiped away,
As the pearl gates swing,
And the gold harps ring,
And the sun unsheathe for aye.

Copyright, 1875, by John J. Hood.

The Silver Trumpet. 163

Rev. E. I. D. Pepper, D D. Numbers x. 1, 2. Joel ii. 1. Dr. H. L. Gilmour

1. Hark! hark! loud, long, melodi-ous, The Silver Trumpet swells and falls:
2. There stands the hallowed Mercy-seat, Where man is reconciled to God:
3. There 'mid the sheen of angels' wings The glory of the Lord doth flame:

Its clarion notes are calling us To stand within Jehovah's walls.
Where God is waiting us to greet With pardon thro' the streaming blood.
While God's own voice the message brings Of peace and joy thro' his own name.

1. Jehovah's walls.

CHORUS.

We come! we come! O gracious One! We crowd thy courts with high acclaim! We press around thy great white throne! And shout aloud our Saviour's name!

Saviour's name.

4 No longer hangs the hiding vail:
   No longer is a priest required: [vail.
   Our Great High Priest doth now pre-
   The One by nations long desired.

5 No sacrifice does God demand,
   T' atone for sins of crimson dye:
   No offering from one scarlet hand,
   As, penitent, we now draw nigh.

6 The Lamb of God hath shed his blood:
   It sprinkles now the Mercy-seat:
   Thro' that we may approach to God,
   And in his presence gladly meet.

7 Then let the Silver Trumpet's call
   Stir all our hearts to gather near;
   Before his gracious throne we'll fall,
   And, saved, before his face appear.

Copyright, 1889, by H L. Gilmour.

168. The Beautiful Land.

FANNY J. CROSBY.   JNO. R. SWENEY.

1. We have heard of a land on whose blue, ether skies Not a cloud for a moment can stay, And it needs not the sun in his splen-dor to rise, For the Lord is the light of its day; We have heard of that land, and its glo-ry we seek, Where the faith-ful with heard

2. We have talked of that land when our jour-ney was long, And our hearts overburdened with care, We have talked of the blest at the riv-er of song, And how oft we have sighed to be there; And our faith has gone up, like a bird on the wing, To that land on e-

3. We are near-ing that land, we are near-ing the gate To the cit-y of jas-per and gold, Where the Saviour to welcome his children doth wait, And will gath-er them in-to the fold; To the fold of his love, in the mansions a-bove, Where for-ev-er with

Copyright, 1890, by Jno. R. Sweney.

The Beautiful Land.—CONCLUDED.

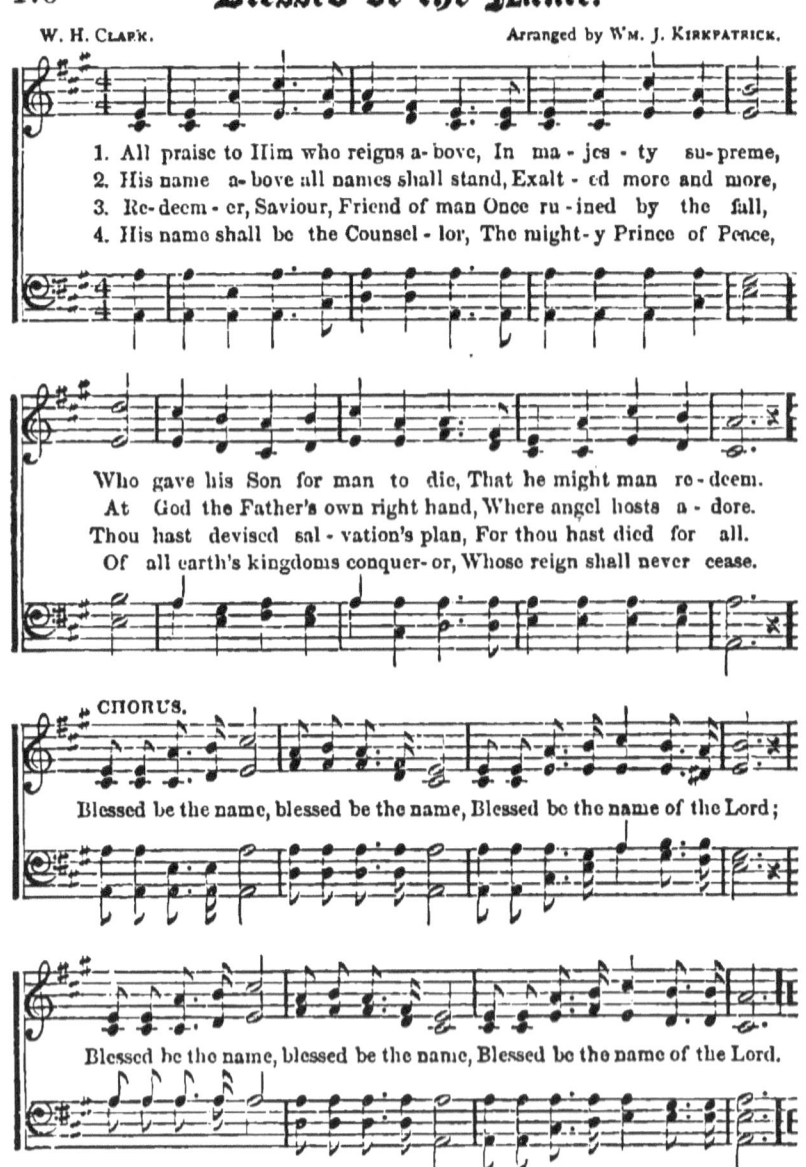

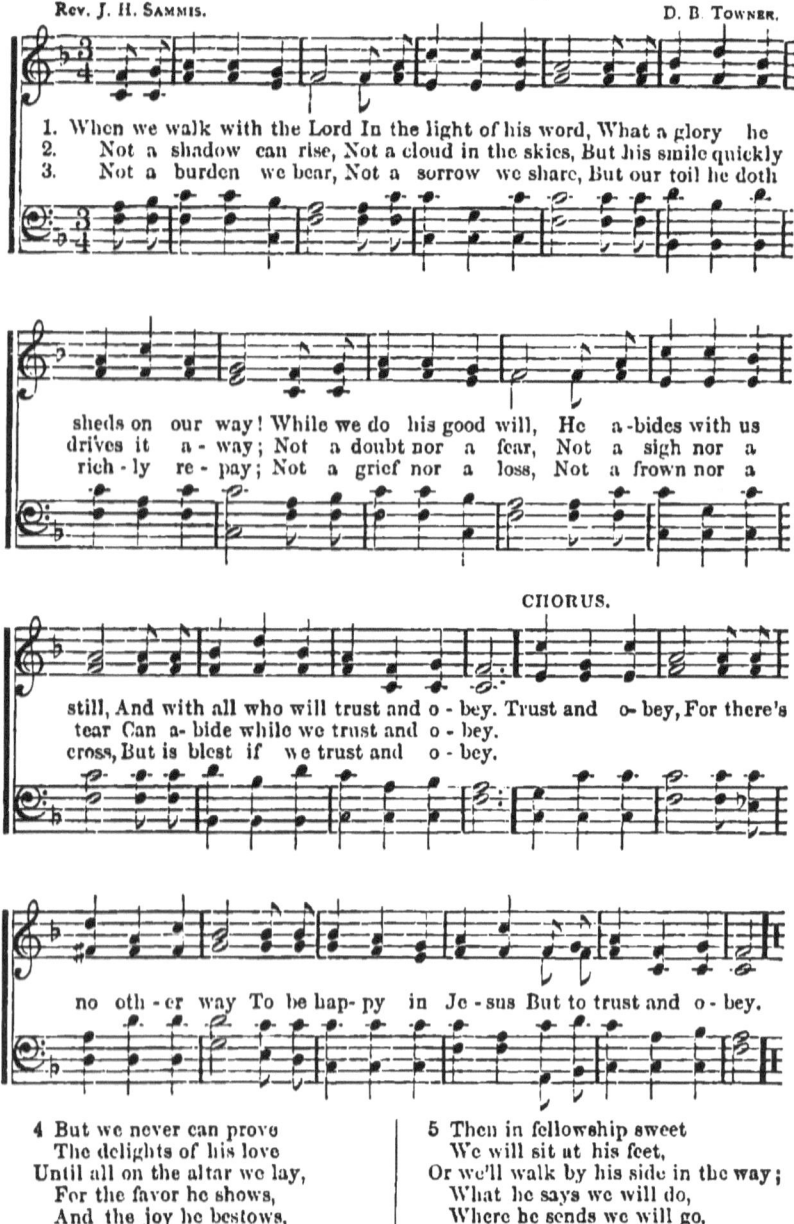

4 But we never can prove
The delights of his love
Until all on the altar we lay,
For the favor he shows,
And the joy he bestows,
Are for all who will trust and obey.

5 Then in fellowship sweet
We will sit at his feet,
Or we'll walk by his side in the way;
What he says we will do,
Where he sends we will go,
Never fear, only trust and obey.

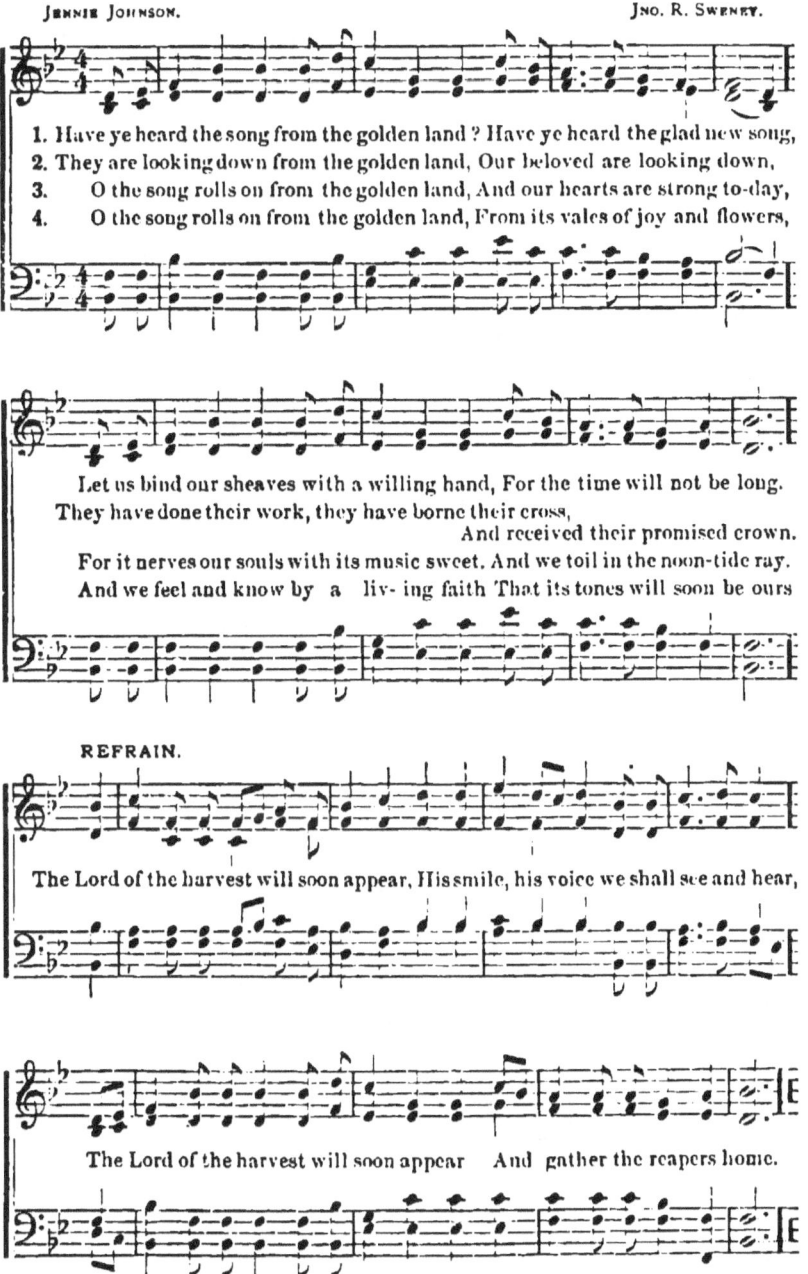

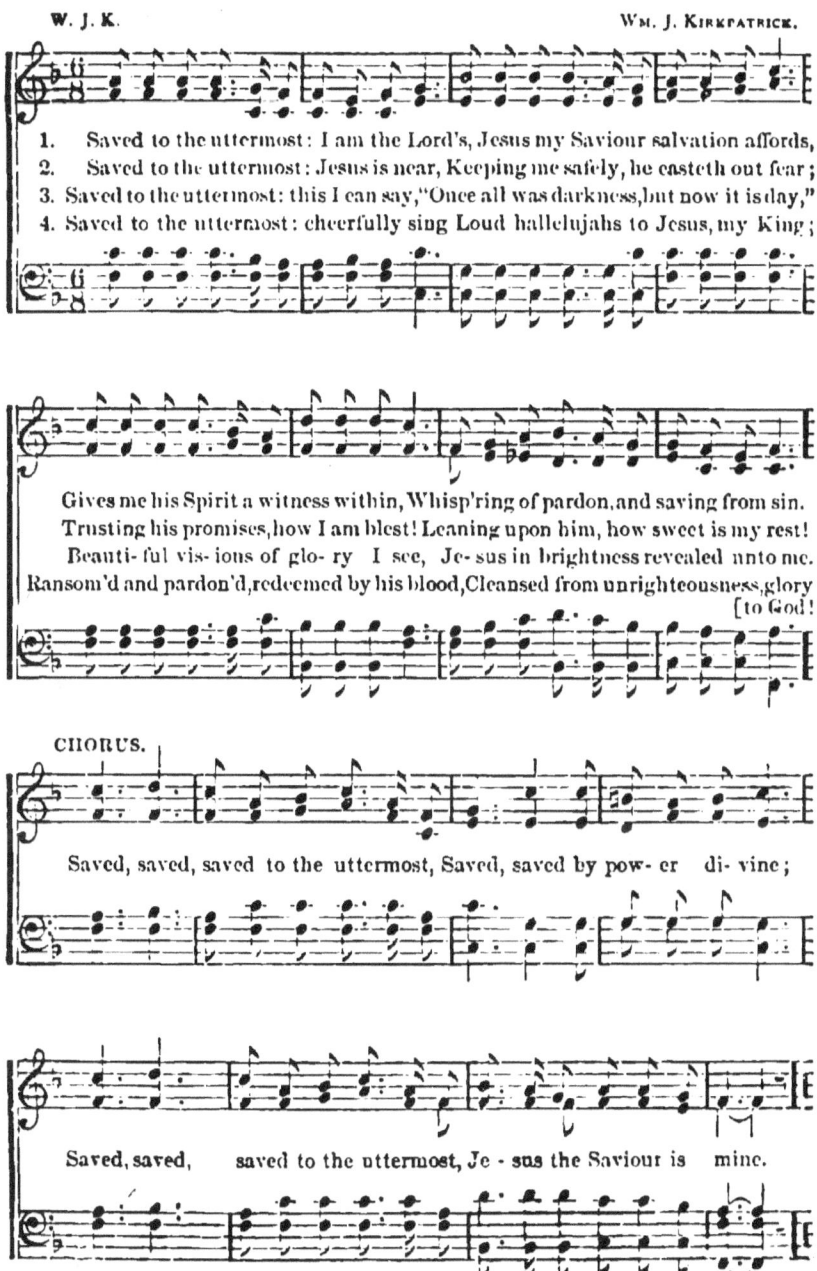

182. Help Just a Little.

Music from "The Wells of Salvation," new words by Rev. W. A. Spencer.
Wm. J. Kirkpatrick.

1. Brother for Christ's kingdom sighing, Help a lit-tle, help a lit-tle;
2. Is thy cup made sad by tri-al? Help a lit-tle, help a lit-tle;
3. Though no wealth to thee is giv-en, Help a lit-tle, help a lit-tle;

Help to save the mil-lions dy-ing, Help just a lit-tle.
Sweet-en it with self-de-ni-al, Help just a lit-tle.
Sac-ri-fice is gold in heav-en, Help just a lit-tle.

CHORUS.

Oh, the wrongs that we may righten! Oh, the hearts that we may lighten!

Oh, the skies that we may brighten! Helping just a lit-tle.

4 Let us live for one another,
  Help a little, help a little;
  Help to lift each fallen brother,
  Help just a little.

5 Tho' thy life is pressed with sorrow,
  Help a little, help a little;
  Bravely look t'ward God's to-morrow,
  Help just a little.

Copyright, 1885, by John J. Hood.

183. I'll Live for Him.

C. R. Dunbar.

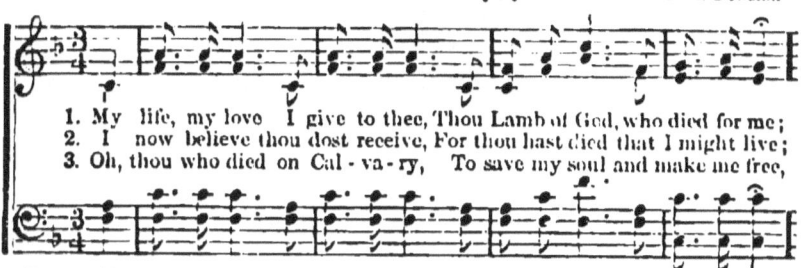

1. My life, my love I give to thee, Thou Lamb of God, who died for me;
2. I now believe thou dost receive, For thou hast died that I might live;
3. Oh, thou who died on Cal-va-ry, To save my soul and make me free,

Cho.—I'll live for him who died for me, How happy then my life shall be!

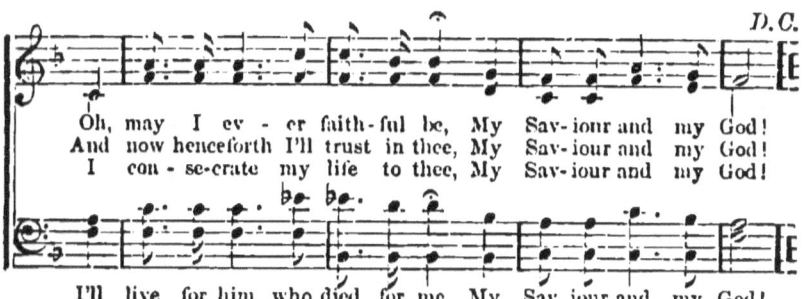

Oh, may I ev - er faith-ful be, My Sav-iour and my God!
And now henceforth I'll trust in thee, My Sav-iour and my God!
I con - se-crate my life to thee, My Sav-iour and my God!

I'll live for him who died for me, My Sav-iour and my God!

184. He is Calling.

Arr. by S. J. Vail.

1. { There's a wideness in God's mercy, Like the wideness of the sea:
   { There's a kindness in his justice Which is more than } li - berty.

CHORUS.

He is call-ing, "Come to me!" Lord, I'll glad-ly haste to thee.

2 There is welcome for the sinner,
   And more graces for the good;
  There is mercy with the Saviour;
   There is healing in his blood.
3 For the love of God is broader
   Than the measure of man's mind;

And the heart of the Eternal
   Is most wonderful and kind.
4 If our love were but more simple,
   We should take him at his word;
  And our lives would be all sunshine
   In the sweetness of our Lord.

185. The Gospel Feast.

CHARLES WESLEY.
Cho. by H. L. G.
"Come, for all things are ready."
Luke xiv. 16.
H. L. GILMOUR.

1. Come, sinners, to the gos-pel feast; It is for you, it is for me;
2. Ye need not one be left behind, It is for you, it is for me;
Let ev'-ry soul be Jesus' guest: It is for you, it is for me.
For God hath bid-den all mankind, It is for you, it is for me.

D.S.—O wea-ry wand'rer, come and see, It is for you, it is for me.

CHORUS.
D.S.

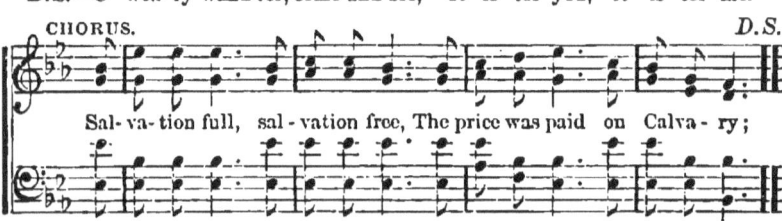

Sal-va-tion full, sal-vation free, The price was paid on Calva-ry;

3 Sent by my Lord, on you I call;
The invitation is to all:
4 Come, all the world! come, sinner, thou!
All things in Christ are ready now.
5 Come, all ye souls by sin oppressed,
Ye restless wanderers after rest;
6 Ye poor, and maimed, and halt, and blind
In Christ a hearty welcome find.

7 My message as from God receive;
Ye all may come to Christ and live:
8 O let this love your hearts constrain,
Nor suffer him to die in vain.
9 See him set forth before your eyes,
That precious, bleeding sacrifice:
10 His offered benefits embrace,
And freely now be saved by grace.

Copyright, 1889, by H. L. Gilmour.

186. There is a fountain. Key A.

1 There is a fountain ‖:fill'd with blood,:‖
Drawn from Immanuel's veins,
And sinners, plunged ‖: beneath that
Lose all their guilty stains. [flood,:‖
CHO.—Oh, glorious fountain!
Here will I stay,
And in thee ever
Wash my sins away.

2 The dying thief ‖: rejoiced to see :‖
That fountain in his day,

And there may I, ‖: though vile as he,:‖
Wash all my sins away.
3 Thou dying Lamb, ‖: thy precious
Shall never lose its power, [blood :‖
Till all the ransomed ‖: Church of God:‖
Are saved to sin no more.
4 E'er since by faith ‖: I saw the stream :‖
Thy flowing wounds supply.
Redeeming love ‖: has been my theme,:‖
And shall be till I die.

187 Ishi.

Cho. by H. L. G.   Hosea 2: 16.   Adapted by H. L. Gilmour.
BARTIMEUS.

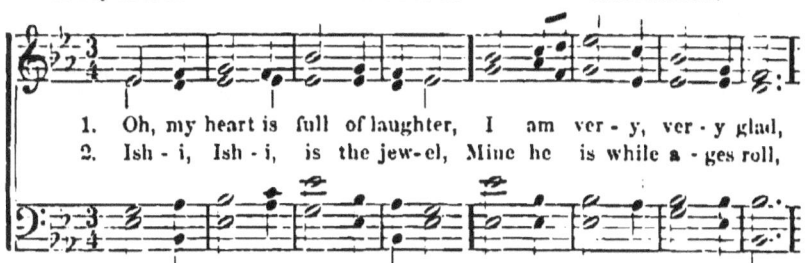

1. Oh, my heart is full of laughter, I am ver-y, ver-y glad,
2. Ish-i, Ish-i, is the jew-el, Mine he is while a-ges roll,

Cho.—Wilt thou have this precious "Ishi" Bridegroom of thy soul to be?

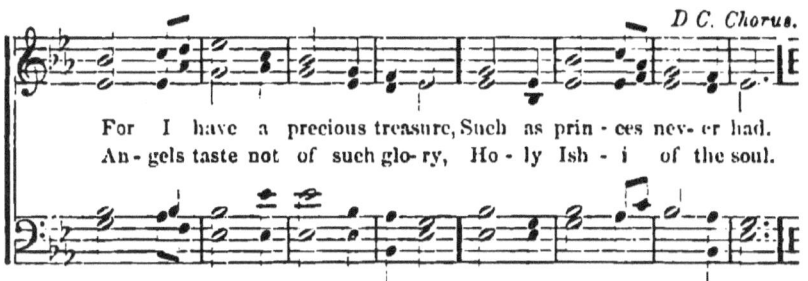

D. C. Chorus.

For I have a precious treasure, Such as prin-ces nev-er had.
An-gels taste not of such glo-ry, Ho-ly Ish-i of the soul.

He, the fair-est of ten thousand, Waits in love to welcome thee.

3 Many beauteous names thou bearest,
Brother, Shepherd, Friend and King,
But they none unto my spirit
Such divine support can bring.

4 Other joys are short and fleeting,
Thou and I can never part,
Thou art altogether lovely,
Ishi, Ishi of my heart.

5 In thy own fair realms of glory,
In the holiest above
Choirs of angels chant the story
Of the wondrous, matchless love.

6 All my longings are contented,
All my wanderings turn to thee,
Pole-star of my restless spirit;
Ishi, all in all to me.

Copyright, 1891, by H. L. Gilmour.

---

188   God is Love.   Tune above.

1 God is love; his mercy brightens
All the path in which we rove;
Bliss he wakes, and woe he lightens;
God is wisdom, God is love.

2 Chance and change are busy ever;
Man decays, and ages move;
But his mercy waneth never·
God is wisdom, God is love.

3 E'en the hour that darkest seemeth
Will his changeless goodness prove;
From the gloom his mercy streameth;
God is wisdom, God is love.

4 He with earthly cares entwineth
Hope and comfort from above;
Every where his glory shineth;
God is wisdom, God is love.

189. At the Cross.

R. Kelso Carter. From "Songs of Perfect Love," by per.

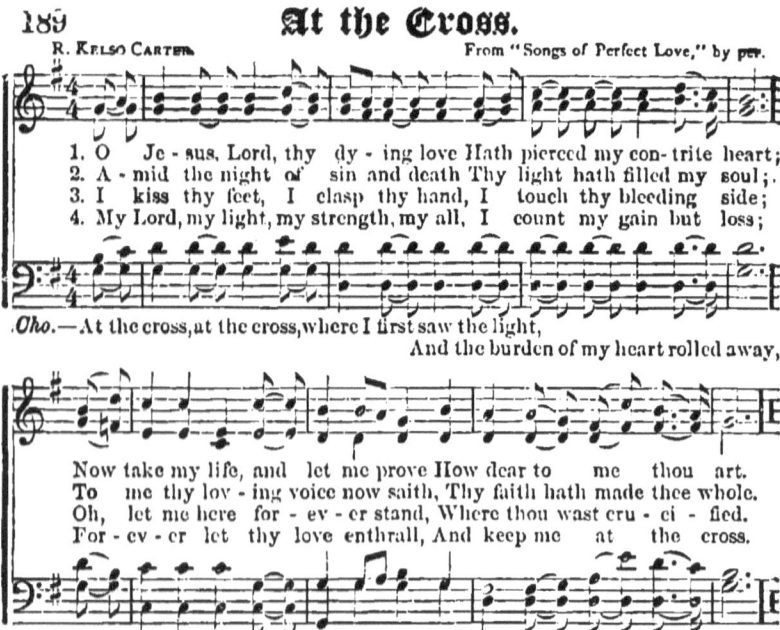

1. O Jesus, Lord, thy dying love Hath pierced my contrite heart;
2. A-mid the night of sin and death Thy light hath filled my soul;
3. I kiss thy feet, I clasp thy hand, I touch thy bleeding side;
4. My Lord, my light, my strength, my all, I count my gain but loss;

Cho.—At the cross, at the cross, where I first saw the light,
And the burden of my heart rolled away,

Now take my life, and let me prove How dear to me thou art.
To me thy loving voice now saith, Thy faith hath made thee whole.
Oh, let me here for-ev-er stand, Where thou wast cru-ci-fied.
For-ev-er let thy love enthrall, And keep me at the cross.

It was there by faith I received my sight, And now I am happy night and day!

190. Cleansing Wave.

Mrs. J. F. Knapp. By per.

1 Oh, now I see the cleansing wave!
The fountain deep and wide;
Jesus, my Lord, mighty to save,
Points to his wounded side.

Cho.—The cleansing stream I see, I see!
I plunge, and oh, it cleanseth me!
Oh, praise the Lord! it cleanseth me;
It cleanseth me—yes, cleanseth me.

2 I rise to walk in heaven's own light,
Above the world of sin, [white,
With heart made pure, and garments
And Christ enthroned within

3 Amazing grace! 'tis heaven below
To feel the blood applied;
And Jesus, only Jesus, know,
My Jesus crucified.

191. Jesus, I Come to Thee.

FANNY J CROSBY.   WM. J. KIRKPATRICK.

1. Je-sus, I come to thee, Longing for rest; Fold thou thy wea-ry child Safe to thy breast. Rocked on storm-y sea,
2. Je-sus, I come to thee, Hear thou my cry; Save, or I per-ish, Lord, Save, or I die.
3. Now let the roll-ing waves Bend to thy will, Say to the troubled deep, Peace, peace, be still.
4. Swiftly the part-ing clouds Fade from my sight; Yon-der thy bow ap-pears, Love-ly and bright.

CHORUS.

Oh, be not far from me, Lord, let me cling to thee, On-ly to thee.

Copyright, 1884, by John J. Hood.

192. Nearer, My God! to Thee.

1 Nearer, my God! to thee,
Nearer to thee!
E'en though it be a cross
That raiseth me!
Still all my song shall be,
Nearer, my God! to thee,
Nearer to thee!

2 Though like the wanderer,
The sun gone down,
Darkness be over me,
My rest a stone,
Yet in my dreams I'd be
Nearer, my God! to thee,
Nearer to thee!

3 There let the way appear,
Steps unto heaven;
All that thou sendest me,
In mercy given;

Angels to beckon me
Nearer, my God! to thee,
Nearer to thee!

4 Then, with my waking thoughts
Bright with thy praise,
Out of my stony griefs
Bethel I'll raise;
So by my woes to be
Nearer, my God! to thee,
Nearer to thee!

5 Or if, on joyful wing
Cleaving the sky,
Sun, moon and stars forgot,
Upward I fly,
Still all my song shall be,
Nearer, my God! to thee,
Nearer to thee!

INDEX.

Titles in CAPITALS; Metrical Tunes in *Italic*; First lines in Roman.

HYMN.		HYMN.		HYMN.	
Alas! and did my Sav-.	82	FAIR PORTALS.	86	I know in whom my soul	78
A light o'er my pathway	32	Falter not nor look be-.	119	I know not the hour of.	134
All for Jesus! all for	35	Father above, a blessing	42	I'LL LIVE FOR HIM.	183
All glory to my Sav-	151	FILL ME NOW.	193	I'm helpless, Lord,	161
ALL IS LOVE.	33	Fill this temple with thy	104	IMMANUEL'S LAND.	130
All praise to Him who	170	FIRM TO THE END.	95	INFINITE LOVE,	32
ALL TO THEE.	65	FOR JESUS.	107	In the glory of the.	71
ANCHORED ON THE R..	62			In the good old way	41
Anywhere with Jesus	67	GATHER THE REAPERS	175	In the time of trouble,.	83
Are you happy in the	176	GLORIOUS AS THE	58	Into the fountain of	57
A SONG OF JOY,	89	Glory be to the Father,.	194	IS HE,	187
As the bird flies home	12	GLORY, I'M REDEEMED.	9	Is it well with thee?	88
AS WE ARE KNOWN.	31	Glory to Jesus, who died.	171	IT IS TIME TO SEEK	148
AT THE BREAKING OF.	90	GLORIA PATRI.	197	It needs but a touch,	116
AT THE CROSS.	189	God is love; his mercy	188	I WILL SHOUT HIS	154
AT THE SETTING OF	28	God is visiting his peo-.	77		
AT THE THRESHOLD.	84	GOING HOME TO GLO-.	106	Jesus calls, your heart	84
A voice is heard in the.	46	Go on with the work, go	73	Jesus, I come to thee,	191
Awake, awake! the	51	Go when the daylight is	63	Jesus is calling thee!	149
		GRACE IS OVERFLOW-.	50	JESUS IS C. FOR THEE..	56
BEAUTIFUL ROBES.	156	Gracious Lord, for thy	65	JESUS OF NAZARETH	161
BE OF GOOD CHEER.	97			JESUS SAVES,.	173
BE OF GOOD COURAGE.	98	Hallelujah, praise to Je-	33	Jesus saves me and	178
Blessed assurance,	167	Hark! hark! loud, me-.	163	Jesus the Saviour is call-	66
BLESSED BE THE	170	HASTEN THY KINGDOM	34	JOY IN ZION,	140
Blessed Saviour, look	23	Have ye heard the song	175		
BLESS US NOW.	49	Have you carried cups.	124	KEEP CLOSE TO THE	53
Breaking through the	18	Have you heard the in-.	122	KEEP MY SABBATHS, .	105
BRIGHTER EVERY DAY.	37	HEAR AND ANSWER	155		
BRIGHT STARS OF PRO-	114	Hear the voice of the Sa-	127	Lay aside thy fears, O	10
Bring your vessels not	50	HEAVEN IN THE	8	Lead me, ever lead me,.	147
Brother for Christ's king-	182	Heavenly Father, we thy	49	LEAD ME, SAVIOUR.	165
BROUGHT BACK. .	43	He feedeth his flock like	29	LEAD THEM TO THE	7
		He healeth the broken	69	LEANING ON THE EV-	44
Can a boy forget his	15	HE IS CALLING.	184	Leaving all to Jesus!	91
Christian, to the rescue!.	137	HE'LL WIPE THE .	68	LET THE BLESSED	181
CHRIST'S INVITATION.	127	HELP JUST A LITTE.	182	Let the children of Zion	140
CLEANSING WAVE.	190	HIS BLOOD WASHES	178	LET THE LIGHT	59
CLINGING TO THEE.	42	HIS LOVE PASSETH	92	Let "the wings of the	55
COME HOME.	22	HOLDING ON TO JESUS.	20	Let us carry the sun-	72
Come, sinners, to the gos-	187	HOLD OUT THE HAND.	118	Lift your eyes to the	45
Come, sinners, to the Liv-	185	Hold up the Bible, for	60	Light is spreading,	99
Come to the cross, thy	126	Holy, holy, holy ; angel	3	LIGHT OF THE WORLD,.	75
COME TO THE FEAST. .	122	Hover o'er me, Holy	193	LIKE AS A FATHER,	80
Come to the Saviour,	54	How can I honor him?.	135	LIVE IT OUT..	11
COME TO THE SAV-	66	However weak your faith	11	Lo, I am with you al-	128
COME UNTO ME. .	48	How restless the souls .	43	LOOKING AWAY TO JE-	27
		HUMBLY TRUSTING,	23	Lord Jesus, I come in	85
Delay not to come to	153			LOVE FOUND ME, .	152
DO IT NOW. .	177	I am holding on to Je-	20		
Don't let it be said, too.	19	I am praying, blessed	155	MEET ME THERE..	166
Do you feel your load of	103	I AM SAFE,	112	MINE EYES SHALL BE-.	134
Do you hear that gentle.	81	I am walking with my	121	More about Jesus would	180
Doxology.	194, 195, 196	I come with aching	93	MY LEADER,.	96
DRINKING AT THE LIV-	55	I found the love that	115	My life, my love, I give.	183
		If the cup of life that you	98	My soul, in sad exile,	158
EVERLASTING LIFE	123	I follow the footsteps of.	39	MY SPIRIT IS FREE,	39
Every one may have a	113				

RADIANT SONGS.

Title	No.
Nearer, my God ! to	192
New songs, new songs	129
NEVER A DAY SO SUN-	52
NEVER DESPAIR, O B.	129
NO BETTER FRIEND.	17
NO KING BUT CHRIST,	24
NO VOICE BUT THINE,	101
Not one thing hath	117
O BLESSED WAY,	144
O come, to Calvary turn-	56
O'er the rapid stream I	64
Oft' when tossed on o-	112
O happy day, that fixed	183
Oh, how oft amid our	90
Oh, my heart is full of	187
Oh, now I see the cleans-	190
Oh, the night of time	25
Oh, wondrous love !	123
O Jesus, Lord, thy dy-	189
Old Hundred, L. M.	196
O, let the light stream in	59
On life's great battle	97
Only for Jesus, the lives	100
On the cold, barren hills	164
On the desert mountain.	111
On the happy, golden	166
On the Saviour I've be-	9
On to the battle front,	47
One thing I know; oh,	142
O PRECIOUS JESUS !	141
O stay not, O stay not,	109
O THAT BEAUTIFUL	64
O the harvest days are	28
Our friends on earth we.	145
Out in the sunshine of	74
O, work for the Master;	138
Peace, said the Master	21
Praise God, from	195, 196
PRAISE THE LORD FOR	164
PRAISE, PRAISE HIS	111
Praise to thee, Mighty	132
Prayer is the key,	157
PRAYING FOR ME,	181
Precious Jesus, I am	141
PURITY, WHITER THAN	57
PUT MY NAME ON THE.	108
Rejoice in the Lord, O	4
REMEMBER THE SAB-	61
RESCUE THEM,	137
Resting in the love of	62
Ringing, ringing, sweet-	146
Safe in the glory land,	41
Saved to the uttermost;	179
Save now, O Lord, S. M.	93
Saviour, lead me, lest I	165
Send the tidings, happy,	14
SEND THE LIGHT,	110
Serve the Lord with	13
Sessions, L. M.	195
Sing, O sing the love of.	102
Sighing amidst the shad-	129
Sinners, turn ; why will	76
Sinner, while in careless	26
Soldiers of Jesus, who	34
Soldiers ot th' Sunday-	105
SOMETIME,	46
Speak to me, Jesus, I'm	133
Standing on the prom-	172
STEPPING IN THE	182
Sun of righteousness di-	75
SUNSHINE IN THE SOUL	159
Sweet the moments,	160
Swing back for one mo-.	86
TELL IT OUT WITH G.	176
THAT GENTLE WHIS-	81
THE BALM OF THE	63
THE BEAUTIFUL LAND,	168
THE BLOOD IS ALL MY.	82
THE EAERLASTING	3
THE FOUNTAIN OF	54
THE GOLDEN KEY,	157
THE GOSPEL BELLS,	146
THE GOSPEL FEAST,	185
The great day is nearing	16
THE HAVEN OF REST,	158
THE MORNING LIGHT,	25
THE RAINBOW ROUND.	36
The Saviour invites you,	22
THE SILVER TRUMPET,	163
The sweetest song my	82
THE WINGS OF MORN-	55
THE WONDROUS LOVE,	115
There are thousands	5
There is a fountain	182
There is joy in my soul,	96
There is joy within when	72
There is work for one	177
There's a call comes	110
There's a hand held out	182
There's a " heaven in	8
There's a promise for	114
There's a wideness in	184
There's never a day so	52
There's no better friend,	17
There's sunshine in my	159
The Sabbath comes,	61
The sands of time are	130
THE VERY SAME JESUS,	7
THE WALK TO EM-	125
The way grows brighter	37
THE WONDROUS STORY	70
This life is like a vapor,	53
'TIS ONLY TO THEE,	130
'TIS SUMMER IN MY	78
'Tis the blessed Saviour	48
'Tis the Lord's own hand	96
Thou art, O Lord, the	144
TRUST AND OBEY,	174
TRUST AND TRY,	136
Trust the Lord, for he	136
Trying to walk in the	175
Use me, O my gracious.	143
WALKING IN WHITE,	121
We are banden together	95
We are going home to	106
We are singing on the	120
We come again,	101
We find in the valley of	79
We have heard a joyful,	173
We have heard of a land	168
We have walked with	125
WE'LL NEVER SAY	145
WELLS IN THE VAL-	79
We shall know as we	31
We shall walk with him.	156
We walk by faith, and	38
We want to live for Je-.	107
We will help one an-	94
We will sing the blessed	70
What a fellowship, what	44
When darkness shrouds	68
WHEN EACH OTHERS.	71
When out in sin and	152
When shall we all meet.	139
When silent falls the	80
When the clouds hang	36
When the jewels of	58
When weary and worn	130
When we walk with the.	174
WHERE DO YOU JOUR-.	150
WHICH WILL YOU C.	26
While these favored	148
Whither do you journey	150
Who'll enroll his name.	108
Who stands outside the	181
Why stand we here idle ?	6
Why will ye die,	40
WILL YOU RISE ?	103
Ye armies of the living	24
YE HAVE DONE IT UN-.	124
You ask what makes me	154
You've read what our	118

(192)

www.ingramcontent.com/pod-product-compliance
Lightning Source LLC
Chambersburg PA
CBHW020829190426
43197CB00037B/741